HOW TO
SELL YOUR HOUSE

by
Harley Bjelland

A Step-by-Step Guide To Help You Sell Your House *Fast,* For The *Best Price,* and *Pocket* The Broker's Commission.

Published by Cornerstone Library
A Simon & Schuster Subsidiary of
Gulf & Western Corporation

Simon & Schuster Building
1230 Avenue of the Americas
New York, New York, 10020

The trademark of Cornerstone Library, Inc. consists of the words "Cornerstone Library" and the portrayal of a cube and is registered in the United States Patent Office

ISBN 346-12381-X

To Foster-Harris, Mentor.

PREFACE

This book provides the average homeowner with an easy-to-understand, step-by-step guide for selling their own home without the use of a broker or real-estate salesperson.

You need not be a real estate expert to sell your own home. The procedures for selling a house have become so routine, so standardized that most home sales can be handled by an average person, with little or no knowledge of real estate.

If you want to save thousands of dollars, get the right price for your home and sell it quickly, this book will literally take you by the hand and lead you through the ten steps needed to prepare, sell and close the sale of your home.

And, the cost of this book is tax deductible from the profits you'll make in the sale of your house.

CONTENTS

HOW TO
SELL YOUR HOUSE

1
TEN STEPS TO SELL YOUR HOUSE

You *can* sell your own house and earn an extra $2,000, $4,000, $6,000 or more, even though you don't know anything about real estate.

If you hire a broker to sell your house, you will have to pay the broker 6 percent of the sales price of your house out of *your profits*. On a $40,000 house, you hand over $2,400 out of *your profits* to a realtor or broker. On a $72,000 house, you'll net only $67,680 and pay your realtor $4,320. On a $100,000 house, $6,000 is taken out of your profit by the realtor and you'll net only $94,000 on the sale. These figures are based on a 6 percent commission. In some cities the realtor's commission has risen to 7 percent, so your profits could be even less.

Don't deceive yourself and say the buyer pays the realtor's fee. The buyer doesn't! *You* pay the fee. *You* hired the realtor and *you* must pay the realtor out of *your* profits.

If you sell your house by yourself, *you* pocket all of the profits. It's *your profit*, to have and to hold. You can bank it, invest it as a down payment on another house, take a trip to Europe, buy a car, do whatever you wish with this money bonanza.

Just think how long it took you to save your last $5,000!

DON'T I NEED TO BE A REAL ESTATE EXPERT?

"But I don't know anything about real estate," you may protest. "I don't know a trust deed from a lien, and I have no idea of the work required to sell my own home. Besides, I'm a little afraid to try. Real Estate has always seemed like such a mystery to me."

Let me attack that 'mystery' objection first. The real estate professiom, as is true of so many businesses, creates its own peculiar, self-serving vocabulary so that only the *in* people can speak and understand their language. Doctors, engineers, lawyers, politicians, all workers create a special language which the average person doesn't understand.

I'm going to take the mystery out of the real estate language and translate the confusing jargon so that an average homeowner can understand all of the important words used. In the *Glossary* (pages 163-172) I have arranged alphabetically and translated real estate jargon into the language an average homeowner can understand.

Let me give you an example. Many people are confused by the difference between a broker and a realtor. The distinction is really quite easy to understand. A *broker* is a person, licensed by the state, who sells real estate for a commission. A *realtor* is a person who is not only licensed by the state to sell real estate for a commission, but who also belongs to the National Association of Realtors. As a member of NAR, the realtor has to live up to a strict code of ethics which protect both the buyer and the seller.

So, a broker is *any* person who is licensed by the state to sell real estate. And a realtor is a broker who must live up to a strict code of ethics.

You may run across a few other words you don't understand in this book. I've stayed away from real estate jargon as much as possible, but if any words have slipped in which you don't understand, look them up in the *Glossary.*

There are an estimated half-million real estate salespeople in the United States. They sell an estimated three-quarters of the 2 million old homes sold each year (2 out of 3 people buy a used home). Who sells these remaining half-million homes?

People like you and I sell many of these. Ordinary homeowners who don't know *earnest money* from a *conveyance*. Every day untrained people sell their own homes, without a real estate agent.

New home construction is down so the market for used homes is increasing, and will continue to increase over the next few years. It is truly a seller's market, buyers are clamoring for houses.

One of my neighbors, who was even more naive about real estate than I, also sold his own house about the same time as I did. He knew so little that when someone made him an offer, neither he nor the buyer knew what to do next. They didn't even know about putting a deposit down on a house, so they merely shook hands on it.

The next day my neighbor and his buyer went down to the escrow company and asked, "What do we do now?" The escrow company took them in hand, told them what to do, and the sale went off without a hitch.

So if my neighbor, who didn't even know what a deposit was, could sell his house in only 2 weeks, I'm convinced that *anyone* can sell a house.

Homeowners are the most qualified people of all to sell their own house. As a homeowner, you're much more anxious to sell your house than a broker. You have more at stake. To a broker you are only *one* of many customers. To yourself you are the *only* salesman selling the most important property in the world. You can devote all of your time, ingenuity, enthusiasm, and effort into selling just *one* house. You're familiar with its assets and, since you've lived in it for some time, you can point out its best features, better than anyone. A realtor sells a *house*, a homeowner sells a *home*.

Is it worth your time? Let's assume you spend 10 hours a week and it takes 2 weeks to sell your $60,000 house. You've earned $3,600, a wage of $180 per hour, a pretty reasonable return for your efforts. And, you've learned a lot in the process.

But, perhaps even most important of all is that you can say with pride and with a justifiable sense of accomplishment, "I sold my own house, all by myself."

When I thought of handing over a $6,000 fee out of my profits to a realtor for selling my house, my wife and I decided to try to sell our own house. We figured we had nothing to lose but some of our time and a few dollars to spend on advertising. What's more, if we failed, we could always turn it over to a realtor after we had at least given it a try.

So we decided to sell our own house. We set a time limit of one month. If we failed to sell within that time, we would hire a realtor.

But I must confess that my first feeling was one of panic. Who were we to think that a couple, completely ignorant in real estate, could actually sell their own house?

First I went to the library and searched for a *How To Sell Your House by Yourself* book. But there wasn't any, so I vowed then and there that once I sold my home, I would write such a book, giving step-by-step instructions which ordinary homeowners could follow in selling their own homes.

In spite of the lack of expert advice, my wife and I sold our own house in 3 weeks at an excellent price. And we sold in a time of high-priced and uncertain mortgage money, and of a slow housing market.

We made mistakes, lots of them, but none were fatal. We learned a lot in the process, and that's what we're going to share with you in this book. We'll take you, an average homeowner, unskilled in real estate, step-by-step, through the process of selling your house. We'll answer your most pressing questions, reassure you when you have self doubts, and provide information where you now have little or none.

If you want to get the most possible money for your house, if you want to sell your home in the shortest possible time, if you want to pocket the realtor's 6 percent commission, then read on and see how it's done.

How To Use This Book

This book is written so you'll use it often, from the initial preparations for selling, through getting your house ready, writing your ads, through all the steps until you've pocketed the money and for reference when you have specific questions. In the final chapter I'll give you some advice on moving yourself, and on tax considerations.

Keep this book by your side, fill in the convenient charts and tables I've provided and make notes to yourself in it. You'll find this book one of the best investments you've ever made. The only commission you'll be paying me for helping you sell your house is the few dollars this book cost. Then, when you've sold your house, and put all the money you saved selling it into the bank, don't forget to deduct the cost of this book from your income tax.

To do this all important selling job the *right* way read this book 3 times. First, read it from cover-to-cover. Don't expect to understand everything the first time through. The first reading will acquaint you with the general contents of the book and it will illustrate the various steps you'll be going through to make a successful sale.

For the second reading, make it more leisurely. As you read each chapter fill in as many of the charts, tables and questionnaires as you can. Again, read it from cover to cover. I, for example, found the *Fact Sheet* to be priceless when talking with prospective customers.

Your third reading will likely be a chapter at a time. For this detailed, intensive reading, go through each chapter slowly, as you are getting ready for each upcoming step covered in that particular chapter. This time, finish filling in all of the blanks you missed in the second reading. Check the items off the lists in this book as you do them, the unchecked items will remind you that you still have them left to do. Keep records in this book. They'll serve you as a record of what was done and will be part of your proof when it comes time to figure out your deductions for computing your income tax.

When you're all finished tell me what you think of this book. Write, in care of the publisher, and they'll forward your compliments or complaints to me. I intend to revise this book periodically. Your comments and suggestions will help form possible future editions.

JUST 10 EASY TO UNDERSTAND STEPS

Before we plunge into the heart and soul of this book, let's take a moment to review the 10 steps you'll go through in the next few months.

STEP 1   *Read this book to learn how to sell your house.*
That one's easy, you're already doing it.

STEP 2   *Get your house ready to sell.*
First you find out what needs fixing, then I'll help you decide what's worthwhile fixing. Finally we'll schedule the work to get it done efficiently.

STEP 3   *Set the 'right' price.*
Yor have to set the 'right' price so that it's high enough to leave a little bargaining room, but still not so high that it'll scare buyers away.

STEP 4   *Advertise effectively.*
Now that you're ready to sell, you learn how to write an eye-catching, customer-pulling ad and put it in the right newspapers. And we'll discuss what other means of advertising to use.

STEP 5 *Show your house effectively.*
There are definite techniques to help you show your house effectively and how to answer buyers' questions. How do you pick out a sincere buyer? Which features of your house should you emphasize?

STEP 6 *How to handle offers.*
Should you take the first offer? How long should you wait for a higher offer? When should you make a counter offer? Which offers should you ignore? How big a deposit should you require?

This step is, of course, one of the most important in the entire sequence, so study it well. I've also included a sample agreement which you and the buyer should sign when you accept the buyer's written offer and the buyer gives you a deposit.

STEP 7 *Help your buyer get a loan.*
Some people may shrug and say getting the loan is the buyer's problem. But if your prospective customer doesn't get a loan, you don't sell your house. It's that simple. So you *can*, and *should* help your buyer get a loan. In Chapter 7 I've included a short, easy-to-understand lesson in home financing.

STEP 8 *Learn about escrow.*
What is escrow? What do they do? Do I need them? How much are they going to charge me? Who pays escrow fees? How long will they take?

STEP 9 *What to do while you wait for escrow to close.*
What are the chances your deal will fall through at this stage? What should I do before the bank appraiser comes?

STEP 10 *Get ready, get set, move.*
In this final chapter I'll give you some hints on moving yourself, an estimate of what it would cost to hire a mover to move you, and how to save money if you hire a mover. Then I'll discuss tax considerations on the beautiful profit you've made.

How Long Will It Take?

That all depends on many things. But you should allow from 1 to 2 months. For best results don't start to advertise any later than 2 months before you're ready to move out. That'll allow you 1 month in which to sell your house and 1 month for escrow.

Don't be afraid you won't have a place to live in if you sell too early. You may be able to work out a long escrow, some can be stretched as long as 6 months, if you need to keep living in your house that long.

Most houses sell in the first 2 months they're on the market. The first month usually brings the best offer. Many people decline the first offer, wait for a better offer, then finally have to come down to and accept a lower offer.

Sure, you may sell your property sooner; as you can see from Figure 3-2, some people do. Some houses are sold on the first day, some during the first week. You may be lucky, but don't count on it.

Remember one important thing about quick sales. Often a quick sale means the property was priced far below the market value. If the seller had set a price a little higher, it may have taken a little longer to sell the house. But the money may well be worth the extra time. You'll have to decide that for yourself.

We sold the first house we owned through a broker. It sold the first day it was on the market, but I soon found out that we could have easily gotten another $4,000 if only we didn't accept the broker's recommended price. The broker wasn't interested in our making more money, he set the price so low that he could make a quick sale. Thus we lost $4,000 and the broker lost only 6 percent of that, or $240. And he made his $2,400 commission for only a couple of hours work.

It's far better for a prospective buyer to see your house while you're still living in it and it's filled with your furniture, your appliances, your dishes, pictures, knick-knacks. The buyer wants to feel your home is ready to move into, and you must do everything you can to support this feeling.

If possible, keep your moving out date flexible. This gives some bargaining room when you get an offer. Some people will pay extra to move in quickly, they're sick and tired of the motel, the small furnished apartment they've been living in temporarily.

Above all, don't panic. Don't be afraid you can't sell your house. Don't let fear pressure you into lowering your price too much. In Chapter 6 I'll give you some hints on ways to make your time flexible, so time won't unduly pressure you.

So there you are, ten steps.

The next chapter covers Step 2. You must decide what you have to do to get your house ready to sell, what improvements are worth making and which aren't.

2
GET YOUR HOUSE
READY TO SELL

One of the biggest mistakes a person can make in selling a house is to think they can sell it without fixing it up. The only type of prospect who'll look at a cluttered, unpainted, untidy house are the bargain hunters.

"Oh, come on," you may protest. "Can't my prospects imagine how nice my house will look when they buy it and fix it up?"

No, they can't. Your house communicates its condition to your prospects through their eyes. If they see many obvious uncared-for items, a broken screen door or a wall with plaster gouged out, they'll assume there are many other unmaintained items which they can't see. This lowers the value of a neglected house even more in their estimation.

In this chapter we'll accomplish 3 major items:

1. Show you how to check your house to see what needs fixing.
2. Help you decide what must be fixed, what can be ignored.
3. Show you how to schedule and get this fixup done in the shortest possible time, and with a minimum expenditure of your time and money.

If you've kept your house in good repair, you'll have little to do. If you haven't, you may have a lot of fixup to do, as I did after raising 5 kids in it.

Remember, whether you're selling your house yourself, or through a broker, you'll still have to fix up your house. You can't avoid this vital fixup step unless you're content to take a big financial loss in your sale.

"One of the keys to getting a fast sale and the top price for your house," experienced real estate people say, "is to have your house and yard spic and span."

When we sold our house, a realty company put on the market another house nearby, the same model and price as ours. But the other house was badly in need of a paint job (we'd painted our outside a year earlier). The front and back yards of the other house were badly in need of refurbishment, full of weeds, the grass raunchy, the shrubs sickly and untrimmed. The realtors tried to sell it for some time, but couldn't. Prospects were insulted and ridiculed the realtors for having the gall to show them such a shoddy house.

After a few weeks of failure they finally gave up, painted the outside of the house, landscaped the yard and the house sold shortly after, for a good price. All that was needed was a couple of hundred dollars investment in fixup materials and some labor.

People make surface judgments on a house just as they make surface judgments about people. If we like what we see on the surface, our first impression is to like what's underneath. So let's make sure the *surface* look of your house is pleasing to the eye.

What Needs Fixing?

Get in your car and drive around your neighborhood. Take a notebook and pencil with you. Pay careful attention to what you see as you cruise around because this is exactly what your prospects will see when they drive up to your house.

Are the lawns and houses well-kept and well-spaced? Are there trees and flowers and green areas? Any swimming pools in the neighborhood? Any parks around? Is the street which fronts your house a busy one?

Next, stop your car and park in the street in front of your house, like prospective buyers will when they see your *For Sale By Owner* sign. Sit in your car and take a critical look. Get your notebook and pencil ready and put yourself in your prospect's shoes. Imagine this is the first time you've ever seen your house.

Remind yourself that *50 percent of the job of selling a house is to make the buyers get out of their cars.* If your house doesn't make a good first impression they'll simply shrug and drive on by.

Does the overall picture of your house and yard look inviting? How about the landscaping? Do the shrubs need trimming? The grass need to be cut? Wouldn't a shrub or two perk it up? How about that hole or bare spot in your front yard? Wouldn't an inexpensive shrub fill it nicely?

And, everybody loves flowers. If you can find a small flat of flowers in bloom, they'll perk up your front yard, give it a lot of color and vitality, make it look inviting. Write everything you think needs to be done, we'll decide later if it should be done.

When I made my own survey, I noticed one of my son's old tennis shoes on the roof, 6 old rolled-up newspapers which had been thrown on the roof by a paperboy, and dozens of rocks of assorted sizes and shapes. And the shrubs needed trimming, and . . .

Make notes and proceed. Get out of your car. Walk with cautious steps toward your house, observing as your buyer will. Look everything over carefully. Does your asphalt driveway need resurfacing where the oil has dripped from your car? Note that.

Does the outside need painting? Touchup? Any loose shingles? Does your TV antenna droop? How about the rain gutters, do they sag? Should you flush them out with the hose? Any nails popping out of the siding? Write it all down.

Check the garage door. If it needs paint to cover those greasy fingerprints, it'll take you only an hour and a quart of paint for a *new* looking garage door.

Walk up the front steps and take a critical look at the front door. At this point your prospect can still decide not to ring your doorbell and walk away.

Is your front door bruised where the kids have kicked it open? Is your porch light askew? Are the drapes soiled? Do the shutters hang crooked? Do the steps squeak?

These are all little things but little things add up to an overall good or bad impression.

Step inside your front door, keep your pad and pencil handy. Did the door squeak when you opened it? Record your first impression as you stepped inside your entryway. Does it seem spacious? Or is it dark and cluttered? Do the rugs need shampooing? Does the entryway need to be cleaned and waxed? Write it down.

How about the walls? Look for fingerprints, grease marks, smudges. Take notes now. Later we'll decide if it's worthwhile painting. Scrubbing is free. But keep in mind that *painting probably increases the sales value of your house more than any other single factor!*

Continue walking through your house. Cover all the rooms in this way. Inspect the walls, the ceiling, the floors of each room. If you spot a leak stain in the ceiling make sure to check the roof to find the leak, if you haven't already done so. Ceiling leaks scare many potential buyers, they fear something more serious is wrong than a simple leak in the roof. A common place for leaks is the flashing (the non-corrosive metal strips) around your chimney. One way to check for leaks is to go up in your darkened attic and look for light leaks during the day. Or you can have someone spray the roof with a hose and locate it.

Does this sound like a lot of work? All we're doing so far is making an inspection. We'll decide later whether to fix it or not.

Look in the closets, cupboards, shelves. Are they crowded, messy? A full or overflowing closet or cupboard gives the impression that the house doesn't have much storage space. Make a note to throw away a lot of the junk you've kept for all these years for no particular reason. Or you could hold a garage sale (more on that in Chapter 9). This is also a good time to donate a lot of your reuseable items to the Salvation Army, Goodwill, or other charitable group.

For the things you must keep, pack your out-of-season clothing, your Christmas decorations, your extra clothes in boxes and store them, neatly, in your garage or basement. You'll be moving soon, anyway, so you're just packing up a little ahead of time. Keep emptying your closets until they're only about one–half to three–fourths full. This gives the impression of having lots of closet space.

Check the knobs, hinges, etc. on all your closets and cupboards. Do the doors swing easily, do they close without having to be kicked? Make a note to oil all the hinges and door mechanisms. Also make a note to put fresh shelf paper in all of your cupboards and shelves.

How about the faucets and commodes? Do they drip constantly? Do the sinks, shower and tub drain properly? Check each one. Drain cleaners are pretty inexpensive. So are faucet washers. If you have a difficult stain in one of your sinks ask the man at the hardware store what will clean it off.

Open the medicine chests. Do they look messy, cluttered? Why not invest 50 cents in a can of white paint and spend a half–hour painting the inside? And by all means throw out all of those medicine bottles you haven't used for years.

Check the drapes and curtains. Should they be cleaned? Washed? Vacuum cleaned? Do the drape pulls need fixing?

Are all the appliances which go with the house working? A prospect making an offer for your house will probably stipulate that all of the built-in appliances be working when they move in. Oil everything that needs it including that noisy exhaust fan over the stove. Make a note to clean your stove and oven. Nothing seems to turn a female prospect away more than a dirty kitchen. Touch up any places on your appliances where the paint has chipped away.

"But I have only a month to get ready," you may be saying and this may sound like at least 100 months of work to get your house ready. It really isn't. You'd be amazed (I certainly was) at the tremendous amount of work you can get done if you organize and schedule it properly. Besides, we haven't decided yet whether to do all of this fixing yet. We're still making our list.

One thing you must decide as you go through your house is which appliances, furnishings, etc. are included in the price of your house. As a general rule, unless you specify otherwise, all items which are physically tied down and not easily moveable (built-ins, light fixtures, wall-to-wall carpeting, TV antenna, etc.) are all considered a part of your house. In the *Fact Sheet* which you'll complete in the next chapter, you'll list the fixtures which go with the house. Some additional items, such as a window air conditioner, a washer, or a refrigerator you should not list. You may be able to use one or more of these in your negotiations to clinch your sale, or you may be able to sell them to your buyer.

Now take a good, long look at your backyard. Does the lawn need to be cut, weeded, fertilized? Does your swing set need fixing, paint, a little oil? How about the back fence, any slats loose, broken or missing? If you have any junk lying around make a note to put it all in a pile and haul it off to the dump.

The kitchen window in many houses looks off into the backyard where the kids play. But when the kids are in school it's nice to be able to look out and see some flowers blooming. Make a note to invest a few dollars in some flats of marigolds or geraniums or other flower which is in bloom. They'll perk up a *blah* backyard.

Finally, go through your basement, attic, garage. Plan on doing a general cleanup here, too. Throw away a lot of the junk you've been hoarding for years, donate the reusables to your favorite charity and get a receipt for them. You may be able to deduct the fair market value of these reusable items from your income tax. And, nicest of all, when you move you won't have all that junk to box up, cart around and store in your new house, or apartment.

Do your workbenches and shelves need to be cleaned up, arranged neatly? Most likely your buyer team will give these areas a thorough inspection. They want a place to put the workbench, plug in the power tools, store the outboard engine. Again these areas should be free of clutter.

Which Repairs To Do, Which To Forget.

3 factors help make these decisions:

1. How much time you have available for fixup (I allowed 1 month and my wife and I did a fantastic amount of work in that time).
2. How much money do you want to invest? (A house in an *average* condition can be fixed up for from $200 to $600;
3. How will it look to your prospect if it's *not* fixed?

The third factor by far outweighs the other two. If it looks bad to the buyer, you'll have a hard time selling.

What's that? You don't know how to fix a faucet? Paint a house? Don't worry, neither did I when I started. But your local bookstore and library have plenty of *How To* books which show you, in considerable detail, how to fix anything imaginable in a house.

You may already know, or you'll have to decide how much time you want (or have available) for fixing up. But the money you can spend is a variable, it's an investment, so let me help you make some of these important money decisions.

Generally any dollar you put into improving the appearance of your house will bring you back $5 to $10 in the sales price. Not a bad investment, is it?

Another important factor to keep in mind is that most of the money you spend for repairs and fixup for the specific purpose of selling your house is deductible from your profit when you invest in another house (more details on this aspect in Chapter 10).

Our house was neat and clean when we showed it. We received many compliments from prospects. I'm sure its appearance generated the 3 offers (and a half dozen additional sincerely interested prospects) we received. We also heard many prospects complain about the audacity of some realtors who showed them through many dirty and shabby houses in our neighborhood.

SOAP AND WATER—YOUR BEST INVESTMENTS

Yes, soap and hot water, liberally and energetically applied, are extremely cheap and your best investment. Scrub down the walls, the counter tops, the stove, the floors. You'll use gallons of this very effective combination.

This is also a good time to put the kids to work. They'll not only help get the work done, it'll also keep them out of the way and busy so they won't keep messing up.

Most of your minor landscaping repairs and maintenance are low in cost. Fertilize everything far in advance of selling so that the *perfume* is gone before you show the house and so that the plants and grass have had time to profit from the nourishment. You can pick up small shrubs cheaply (I got some on sale for as low as 49 cents). Flowers in flats, already in bloom if the season is right, cost only a few dollars. The shrubs and flowers will make your front yard more inviting for someone driving by your home. Remember, you have to make a good first impression to get them out of their cars.

Landscaping, neat and simple, can add hundreds of dollars to your selling price.

Painting the outside of your house is another matter, the decision is more complicated. It will take you a few days to do the walls and trim and the paint will cost anywhere from $50 on up (one gallon of paint covers about 250 square feet). Wood siding, cement block and stucco should be repainted about every 5 years. When you paint such absorbent material as stucco you'll have to buy a lot more paint. If you haven't painted in the last 2-3 years and if your paint looks shoddy, faded or is chipping, count on painting the outside of your house. Again, remember first impressions.

Remember that in houses, as in people, coat of paint can cover a tremendous amount of surface blemishes and imperfections with little cost. A good, thorough paint job can add $2,000 to the sales price of your house, even if your buyer moves in and paints it all over again. Don't buy expensive paint. Your new owner may not like your choice of colors. And don't buy gaudy, bright paint either. Stick to the more conservative colors used in your neighborhood. When we sold our house, we'd painted the outside a year earlier so it looked all right. Inside we painted most of the rooms with lighter colors. It surprised us how much more light and cheery the rooms looked after the new paint job.

So if your house needs paint or if the landscaping needs fixing you'll have to take the time to do it, or get ready for low, even insultingly low offers for your house. You'll probably also get a lot of *eek* looks from prospective buyers. And it could take you 6 months, or longer, to sell your house.

INSIDE YOUR HOUSE

The same general idea holds. Soap and water are your most valuable tools.

Most of the plumbing jobs (putting in new washers, cleaning out the drains), the carpentry fixup (tightening knobs, oiling hinges) and the clean-up of the closets are of little cost consequence. Whatever doesn't look good to the eye *must* be fixed up. I just can't emphasize enough that most of your prospective buyers' impressions will come through their eyes, so everything must *look* good on the surface.

Fixing up the door handles, hinges, etc. are musts. About the only time your prospects will use their sense of touch is for opening doors, cabinets, and closets to peer into. So these should work smoothly, not stick or jam when opened.

Are any of your rooms cluttered and crowded? If so, take any excess furniture, knickknacks, etc. and store them neatly in your basement, attic or garage. Human beings generally like the feeling of spaciousness, uncluttered rooms. Even a small room looks bigger if it's not cluttered with too much furniture.

Do the rugs look dirty or stained? If so, clean them. It's fairly easy and inexpensive to clean rugs with the excellent do–it–yourself cleaners and work–saving machines you can now rent.

If your floors need to be cleaned, waxed and buffed, do this also. You're going to get a lot of traffic through your house when all the prospective buyers walk through, so keep your floors clean. When we sold our house we must have escorted about 60 couples (plus about another 20 realtors) through our home.

You might also want to put in some inexpensive, plastic runners on the pathways over your rugs and floors after you've cleaned them. This will not only protect your cleaning job, it also creates a pleasing atmosphere of cleanliness and neatness which will impress prospective buyers with the tender, loving care you've given your house for all these years.

Before selling our house, we rented a large machine and my wife sanded the 3 wooden floors our kids had used and abused. She then covered them with 2 coats of clear, polyurethane varnish. They looked so beautiful and shiny you could comb your hair in the reflection.

We hired a professional to clean our rugs only because I was working over 50 hours a week at the time and had little spare time. Both the sanding and shampooing were good investments. Many prospects complimented us on the look of our floors and rugs.

How about your curtains and drapes? Wash them and clean them if they need it. If the drape pulls need fixing repair them. You'll likely be opening and closing your drapes for prospective buyers who want to see what's outside your windows. If your drapes are badly worn replace them with inexpensive, ready-made curtains and drapes.

The drapes in our house needed replacement in the 3 kids' bedrooms and in the 2 floor–to–ceiling windows in our living room. The drapes were about 15 years old. We bought inexpensive curtains at a department store for the 5 bedroom windows, and sheer drapes for the living room. All these improvements cost a little over $100—another worthwhile investment which helped us get a good price for our house.

As for closets, cupboards and shelves, new shelf paper costs little and is a must. Use plain, white paper. A gaudy design may turn your customers off.

Finally let's decide whether to paint your rooms. Here again money, time, and appearance are the deciding factors. It costs about $20 to paint an average room (again, don't buy expensive paint, your buyer will probably want another color scheme and paint them all over again). It should take only about a day to paint 2 or 3 rooms with rollers. However, if you're covering a dark color with a lighter one you may need 2 coats. Check with your paint dealer. A coat of darker paint should cover any lighter color. When you paint, pick neutral colors like white, off-white, etc. Nothing too gaudy or bright. Light colors brighten up a room.

Here again you must decide. If the walls don't look good you *must* paint them or suffer the consequences of getting a low price and taking a long time to sell.

HOW TO SCHEDULE YOUR JOBS

By now you have completed your inventory of what *could* be done and have decided what *must* be done. Let's schedule the tasks which *must* be done and put them in the right order so you can get the most work done with the least effort and time. If you schedule these jobs properly you can get a fantastic amount of work done in a short time with no wasted motion or wondering what to do next.

But don't make the mistake of over-estimating what you can get done on a weekend, or in an evening. It's far better to underestimate what you can do and end up ahead of your fixup schedule so you'll have a little time left over to take care of the *OBTW*'s, the *Oh By The Ways*, the jobs you forgot about or didn't complete earlier.

I've divided the tasks into 4 parts, allowing 1 month for the total job. Even if you need more time, or less time, follow this general plan and order. I've arranged the jobs efficiently so you do all the similar tasks in the same day.

You may be able to do the work in less time depending on how many workers you have or the condition of your house. For example, one person could do the First Week's outside work at the same time another person concentrates on the inside work, the Second Week's tasks.

Allow two to four weeks for your fixup, unless you have some major jobs to do.

You might also consider taking a few days of vacation at this time so you can get the necessary work done faster. Or you might hire some of the neighborhood high-school youth to help you.

FIRST WEEK—LANDSCAPING AND OUTSIDE WORK

1. Check rainspouts, gutters, repair
2. Clean all junk off roof, repair loose shingles, straighten TV antenna
3. Do outside painting, touchup
4. Plant new shrubs
5. Plant blooming flowers
6. Trim all shrubs, cut grass, trim edges
7. Fertilize
8. General cleanup of front and backyard, repair fences, etc.
9.
10.

Spend your first week (whether it be nights after work, during the day, or on weekends) doing the outside work. Do any necessary landscaping, outside painting, planting, fertilizing, repair and general cleanup.

Go through the list above. Put the day down you're going to do that specific job, then check it off when you get it done. Cross off whatever tasks you don't need to do and add whatever extra needs to be done. Reading from top to bottom, the jobs are arranged in the order in which they should be done, for example you should clean off the roof and repair the rain gutters before you paint.

You'll find it an excellent idea to work from a checklist such as this. It not only serves as a reminder as to what has to be done next, but you also get a sense of accomplishment out of checking off the jobs, knowing you're that much closer to selling your house.

It's a good idea to get the outside work done first because it not only cheers you up, it will also look good to the neighbors and to potential customers driving by. If your neighbors compliment on how nice your yard and house look, you know prospective customers will

feel the same and you'll be accomplishing that all important first task, getting your prospects out of their car so
they'll come inside your house.

SECOND WEEK—INSIDE CLEANING, PLUMBING AND CARPENTRY

1. Caulk holes in all inside walls, replaster cracks
2. Clean out all closets
3. Clean out cupboards
4. Get ready to paint (wash walls, etc.)
5. Clean out garage
6. Clean out basement, attic
7. Send load of reuseables to your favorite charity
8. Repair all leaky faucets, toilets
9. Oil and repair appliances
10. Clean (and paint if needed) front door
11. Repair doorknobs, oil hinges
12. Fill cracks in basement walls
13.
14.
15.

For your second week move inside. Do your general
major cleanup, uncluttering of closets, donate your reusables to a charity, make all the minor plumbing or
carpentry repairs. Fill in all the nailholes and chipped
plaster areas.

You want to show off your house in its best light, so
put in 100 watt light bulbs everywhere.

Many of these jobs can be done at the same time depending on how many workers you have. You'll be
amazed at what 2 or 3 people, properly organized, can
get done in a week.

THIRD WEEK—INTERIOR PAINTING, MISCELLANEOUS

1. Send drapes out to cleaners
2. Wash curtains

3. Paint rooms
4. Do floors
5. Shampoo rugs
6. Install shelf paper
7. Prepare *Fact Sheet* (covered in Chapter 3)
8.
9.
10.

Before you start painting inside pull down the curtains and drapes which need cleaning and get them out of the way.

After painting and cleanup concentrate on the floors and rugs. Put your plastic runners down if you're going to use them. Finally install new shelf paper and put your things back on their shelves, neatly and orderly. Also start filling in the *Fact Sheet* which is described in the next chapter.

From now on everyone in your house has to be clean and neat. Lay down the law. From here on your house must be clean, orderly, clean, spotless, clean. This may sound as if I have a mania for cleanliness, but I never heard a prospect complain that our house was too clean.

FOURTH WEEK—FINAL TOUCHUP

1. Call or check newspapers for ad requirements (See Chapter 4)
2. Set your price (Chapter 3)
3. Write your ad and place it
4. Hose out garage, basement floor
5. Wash all windows
6. Repair, resurface asphalt driveway
7. Fix drape pulls, put curtains and drapes back up
8. General cleanup, take last load to dump
9. Wash your car
10. Wind up garden hoses neatly
11. Do the *OBTW*'s, the things you forgot or didn't have time for before

12. Dry run through your house
13. Get ready for your rush of buyers
14.
15.
16.

At the beginning of the week call (or check in the want ad section of) your local and metropolitan newspapers. Find out their ad rates so you can write an attractive ad. Read Chapter 4, then place your ad a few days ahead of time. Your ad should start on a Friday night or a Saturday morning.

Now that you have most of your fixup done, you have to set a price. You want to get paid for all the hard work you've done, and for the money you've invested so wisely in your house. Reread Chapter 3 to help you set your price.

Wash all the windows inside and out. Put the clean drapes and curtains back up, fix the drape pulls, finish the general cleanup outside and do all the things you forgot to do or didn't have time to do before.

Make up all of your beds and keep them made up all the time to get in practice for *Show Time* next week. If your bedspreads are worn buy low-cost ones and put them on the beds.

Near the end of the last week both husband and wife should make dry runs, taking turns escorting each other through the house to practice what to say, what to show and do when conducting a real prospect through the home. More on this in Chapter 5.

SHORTCUTS

Suppose you've done your very best but you've just run out of time and money to do any more. Don't panic, there are some shortcuts you can use.

If you've scrubbed a wall in your kid's room and still haven't been able to get rid of that ink stain and you simply don't have the time or money to paint the room you might consider painting only that one wall, if you can get a good match on the paint. Or you could hang a poster or picture over the stain. And you can also hang calendars, knickknacks, or pictures over dirty spots, knocks and scratches on your other walls after you've done your very best to put everything into good shape, but simply ran out of time.

If you have a stain or a tear in your bedspread, cover it with an attractive pillow. For a worn spot on any rugs use a scatter rug. And you can cover a burnspot or stain on your counter top in your kitchen with a sparkling coffee spot or fancy dish.

If you don't have the time and money to paint the entire outside of your house, and if your house isn't too badly in need of paint, consider painting only the front of the house. If you can match the existing paint, it'll perk up the side of your house which is visible from the street.

Now that you've invested your time and money, let's see how to set the price for your home.

3
SET THE RIGHT PRICE

"A house correctly priced is half sold," most real estate experts agree. Setting the *right* price is one of the most important steps you'll take.

"One of the biggest mistakes in selling a house is setting the price too high," is another truism in real estate.

An overpriced house will scare buyers away and take a long time to sell. Buyers ask how long a house has been on the market. If it's been on too long, they'll get suspicious and wonder why it hasn't sold. The longer your house is on the market the harder it is to sell and the more you'll eventually have to come down in your selling price.

If you price your house too low, you're going to cheat yourself out of some money. Besides a low price also makes buyers suspicious. They wonder if the house has some serious, hidden faults, or that you live in an undesirable neighborhood, etc.

So, you must set the *right* price for your house to sell fast and for the most money. Remember, the biggest financial transaction you and most other families face in a lifetime is buying and selling a house. You want to sell at the right price and your customer wants to buy at the right price. In a good house sale both buyer and seller should be satisfied.

But how do you set the right price? How much room should you leave in your price for bargaining? Is an appraisal a must? How long does it usually take to sell a house? What are the best months in which to sell your house?

These and other related questions will be answered in this chapter.

FACT SHEET

Before you set your price you must know exactly what you're selling.

"That's ridiculous," you may object. "I'm just selling my house, aren't I?"

No, there's much more to it than that. You not only have to find out certain basic information about your house before you can set a price, you must also decide what *extras* are included in the price. For example, are your drapes, window air conditioner, garden tools, TV antenna, refrigerator, washer and dryer included in your selling price?

Also, your prospective buyers will ask if the house has insulation, what the electrical capacity of the house is in amperes, what size water heater you have, etc.

So, the next step is to fill out the *Fact Sheet* included as Figure 3-1.

This *Fact Sheet* will answer about 98 percent of the questions prospective buyers will ask when they phone or come to see your house. It will provide information about your neighborhood and community for people from out of town who are not familiar with your area. The *Fact Sheet* will help you write a good, eye–catching ad. And you'll need this information for the mortgage company and for escrow after you've sold your house.

In short, you'll find the *Fact Sheet* the most useful single tool in selling your house.

Following the sample *Fact Sheet* I've included explanatory information on how you can find the answers to the questions asked. The blanks in the sample have numbers in parentheses which relate to the explanation which follows telling you how to find the information or how to figure it out.

The first page includes general information of interest to all prospective customers. The second and third pages provide details about your house, its location, etc.

I've included 3 complete sets of *Fact Sheets*. The first set is the sample I referred to above. The second set you can use as a worksheet when you start locating and recording the information. The third set you should fill out neatly. This is the sheet you will be showing your prospects. Make enough copies of this final set to give to all of your seriously interested customers.

FACT SHEET—ONE

Sample

Address: (1) *3630 Adams Drive*   County: *Polk*

City: (2) *San Dimos*   State: *CA*   Zip: *90742*

Square Footage: (3) *1550*   Lot Size: (4) *70' x 130'*

No. Bedrooms: (5) *4*   No. Baths: (6) *1½*   Age of House: (7) *12 Y.*

(8) *2*   Car Garage: (9) *20' x 22'* Basement: (10) *40' x 30'*

Other Rooms: (11) *Kitchen, Living, Dining, Laundry*

Major Improvements Added: (12) *Rugs—living, dining room and halls*
   (2 years old). G.E. dishwasher (1 year old). Outside paint (1 year
   old). Inside paint (1 month).

Special Features: (13) *View of Bass Lake, walking distance to all*
   schools, located in cul-de-sac; 6 dwarf fruit trees

Items Included in Purchase Price: (14) *Drapes, built-ins, carpeting,*
   TV antenna

Legal Description: (15) *Lot 33 of Tract 24243, as per map*
   recorded in Book 473, pages 10 to 12 inclusive of maps in the
   office of County Recorder of Polk County.

Figure 3-1

Zoning/Building Restrictions: (16) *Zoned single residential family,*

over 1200 square feet

Selling Price: (17) *$73,500*

Terms: (18) *Buyer to obtain loan from Barlow Mortgage Company.*

Owners: (19) *Charles & Marilyn*   Tel.: Home: *253-9846*

Norway   Bus.:   *438-0981, Ext 243*

FACT SHEET—TWO

Sample

Total Rooms: (20) *8*

Room Dimensions: (21)

Kitchen: *10' x 12'*   Bedroom: *1 Master 12' x 15'*

Dining Room: *11' x 11'*   Bedroom: *2 Pink 11' x 12'''*

Living Room: *12' x 20'*   Bedroom: *3 Yellow 11' x 11'*

Family Room: *10' x 14'*   Bedroom: *4 Blue 12' x 11'*

Financial Information: (22)

Current Mortgage(s): *First Mortgage with Barlowe Mortgage Company*
for 42,000 at 6½%. Second mortgage Norman Fed. $6,200 at 6½%.

Monthly Mortgage Payments: (23) *$226 per month first mortgage.*
$39 per month second mortgage.

Taxes Per Year: (24) *$925*   Insurance Per Year: (25) *$128*

Utilities—Average Per Month: (26)

Electricity: *$21*   Fuel: *Not used*   Gas: *$27*

Trash: *$3.00*   Water: *$16*   Other: *none*

General Data:

Air Conditioning: (27) *5 ton cen.*   Heating: (39) *Gas 80,000 BTUs*

Antenna: (28) *Color TV*   Hot Water Tank: (40) *Gas 50 gals.*

Appliances: _____   Insulation: (41) *Ceiling*

   Elec.: (29) *Washer, dryer*   Landscaping: (42) *8 dwarf fruit*

   Gas: (30) *Stove, oven*   Lawn Sprinklers: (43) *Fr. & Back*

Built-ins: (31) *Stove, oven,*   Patio: (44) *10' x 10' concrete*

  dishwasher   Plumbing: (45) *Copper*

Carpeting: (32) *Living, Din. Rms.*   Roofing: (46) *Shingle*

Drapes: (33) *Living, Din. Rms.*   Sewer: (47) *City*

Elec. System (Cap.): (34) *200 amp*   Walls: (48) *Lath and plaster*

  220 V Avail.: (35) *Yes*   Water: (49) *City*

Exterior Const.: (36) *Stucco*

Fencing: (37) *Grape stake*

Fireplace: (38) *Living Rm—Brick*

FACT SHEET—THREE

Sample

Schools:

Elementary—Name: (50) *Pedregal*   Location: *3 Blocks* Grades: *K-5*

Secondary—Name: (51) *Whittier*   Location: *7 Blocks* Grades: *6-8*

High School—Name: (52) *Norman*   Location: *10 Blks.* Grades: *9-12*

Jr. College—Name: (53) *San Dimos*   Location: *3 Miles*

4-Yr. College—Name: (54) *UCLA*   Location: *16 Miles*

   (55) *Catholic School 1 Mile—Grades 1-12*

Shopping Centers: (56) *Grayslake Center—12 Stores—1 Mile*

  San Dimos—50 Stores—3 Miles

Public Transportation: (57) *Bus Stop—6 Blocks*

Facilities:

Churches: (58) *Lutheran, Catholic, Mormon, Seventh Day Adventist*

Hospital(s): (59) *Christensen Memorial—2 Miles*

Fire Station: (60) *1 Mile*   Police Station: (61) *2 Miles*

Post Office: (62) *½ Mile*

Distances to Important Points:

  (63) *San Dimos Freeway—4 Miles*

  Downtown Chinatown—8 Miles

  San Dimos Country Club—1 Mile

Deliveries:

Bottled Water: (64) *Rocky Mt.*   Milk: (65) *Devine Bovine Co.*

Newspapers: (66) *San Dimos Times—Daily, Eldorado Bugle—Weekly*

Trash Pickup: (67) *2*   times per week.

FACT SHEET EXPLANATION

(1) and (2)   Your home address.

(3) The square footage of living area in your house
does not include the garage, basement or attic unless
these areas have been converted into living space
such as for a bedroom, playroom, family room, den,
etc. To get this figure, check the papers you have on
your house, or measure the outside dimensions of the
living area of your house and multiply the two figures
together. In a house 50 feet wide and 31 feet deep, the
area is 50 by 31 or 1550 square feet.

(4) Measure your lot (or obtain the measurement from your house papers) and list as shown. Or, for a larger lot, express in acres, e.g. about 1/2 acre. One acre is 43,560 square feet, that's a square lot 209 by 209 feet. If you're unsure whether to measure the lot depth up to the sidewalk or street you may have to call the County Recorder.

(5) The number of rooms usually used as bedrooms.

(6) A full bath contains a tub, a commode, and a sink as a minimum. A 3/4 bath contains a shower, a commode and a sink. A 1/2 bath contains a commode and a sink. List the total number of baths.

(7) The age of your house in years. If you're not sure and can't find it in your house papers, call the County Clerk's office. They have records on your property from many years back. If all else fails, estimate.

(8) The number of average sized cars your garage will hold.

(9) and (10) List the inside dimensions of your garage and basement.

(11) List all the other rooms including family room, den, recreation room in basement, etc.

(12) What major improvements have you added in the last few years and how old are they? Include drapes, pool, patio, awnings, incinerator, etc.

(13) What special features does your house have, such as a large, central air conditioner, lath and plaster walls, tiled entryway, near golf course?

(14) List all the items which are not easily moveable and are tailor–made for your house, such as venetian blinds, storm windows, screens, light fixtures, window air conditioners, water softeners, etc. Don't list everything you own here, save a few items for your later negotiations. For example, you may want to later consider including your refrigerator, your garden equipment, fireplace equipment, or swing set, etc. in a package deal with your house to clinch the sale. Or you may sell these items separately to your buyer.

(15)   You can find the legal description on the deed to your property, your policy of title insurance, your tax bill, from a subdivision map or from your county recorder. It's vital that this be accurate.

(16)   This information may be in your house papers, or it may have changed, so call the city or county planning department to see how your property is zoned, and what the general building restrictions are.

(17)   This is your *selling price.* Don't even use the word *asking price.*

(18)   Put here any special terms which you would like to make concerning the financing of the sale of your house. For example, the mortgage company who currently holds your mortgage probably has a payoff penalty for paying your loan off in cash, which would happen if your buyer chose another loan company. Typically this is 1 percent of the loan which means $720 could come out of *your* pocket on a $72,000 mortgage if your buyer chooses a different lender. Also, if you're willing to assume a second mortgage state here the size, interest rate and any special conditions, such as a balloon payment at the end of a certain period.

(19)   Husband's and wife's (owners') names, home and business phones.

(20)   The total number of rooms, not including halls, closets, porches, baths, garage or basement.

(21)   Your room dimensions in length by width. Bedrooms may be keyed to color of walls, decorating motif, etc. Don't forget to include special rooms such as a den, recreation room in the basement, etc.

(22)   This is available from either your monthly statements you get from your mortgage company, or call your loan company. It's possible a buyer may be able to pay enough cash down to take over your mortgage directly, but you'd better check with your lender to see if they'll permit this.

(23)   List your first (and second) mortgage payments. If your payment includes insurance and taxes note that here.

(24)   Find this on your yearly tax statement from your loan company, or call your tax assessor. Typically this is 2 to 3 percent of the market value of the house.

(25)   List here if you pay your insurance separate from your mortgage payment. If you don't know what you're paying call your lender or your insurance agent.

(26)   Average your utility bills for the past 6 months or year by checking your past receipts. If you've thrown them away, call the utility company, they should be able to supply the information. It's also a good idea to have copies of past bills to show a doubting, prospective customer. Under *OTHER* list any special monthly payments such as for a sewer assessment, membership in a home association, etc.

(27)   What capacity and type of air conditioner(s) do you have. If you don't have any records on it the nameplate on the unit should tell its capacity, or you can check with the company which services your unit.

(28)   Antenna in attic, rotating antenna, color TV antenna, etc.

(29)   Which of your appliances are electrical?

(30)   Which of your appliances are operated by gas?

(31)   List built-in appliances.

(32)   How much of your house is carpeted? If you have a special carpet material so state.

(33)   How many windows have drapes? If you have a special drapery material, such as non-fading, state that.

(34)   What is the total electrical capacity of your house in amperes? You can find this number on your main circuit breakers, or call the electrical utility which services you and ask them. They should have it on their records, or they can come out and check your

house and tell you. I've personally found the people from the utility companies to be extremely pleasant people to deal with and very helpful.

(35) Is 220 volts available for an electrical dryer or for power tools in the garage?

(36) You may have stucco, wood-frame, brick, stone, aluminum siding, or a combination of these.

(37) What type of fencing do you have and how are the sides of your lot fenced?

(38) It can be brick, stone, or other material, built floor–to–ceiling or shorter.

(39) Heating capacity of your house heater. Get this from the nameplate of your heater, your house records, or ask your utility company to help you find it.

(40) The capacity of your hot water tank should be on the nameplate on your tank, get your flashlight out and read it. Or call the company who sold it, give them the model number and they'll give you the capacity. 30 gallons or more is desirable.

(41) Insulation is most commonly used in the ceiling since from 25 to 40 percent of total heating loss can be through the ceiling. To find out, crawl up into your attic and check for thick, long strips of what looks like cotton batting either on the floor of your attic if your attic is not liveable or stapled or fastened to the ceiling in a liveable attic. To check for insulation in your walls (about 10 to 20 percent of heating loss is through walls), take off a few of the plastic coverplates on some electrical outlets located on outside walls. Slip a screwdriver along the *outside* of the gray terminal box (be careful to not go inside the box or you'll get shocked). Keep pushing your screwdriver in deeper and if you push through something squishy which feels like cotton batting before you reach the solid, outside wall you have wall insulation. Check a couple of other outside wall sockets to be sure.

(42)   Any special landscaping features, such as a lighted fountain, lily pond, or special grass?

(43)   Do you have built-in lawn sprinklers?

(44)   The size of your patio and the type of construction, such as concrete, brick, etc.

(45)   If you have copper plumbing say so. Copper was not introduced until about 1940 and copper plumbing is a very desirable feature. Iron and steel pipes corrode and cut down on water pressure, copper doesn't. To check what you have, use a magnet on your larger pipes in your basement, or under your house. Iron and steel will attract a magnet, copper, bronze or brass won't. If you don't have copper plumbing you may wish to insert some innocuous phrase such as "Easily accessible."

(46)   You have shingles, shake, rock, slate,etc.

(47)   City sewers or a septic tank.

(48)   Wall material: plaster, lath and plaster, hardwood, wallboard, etc.

(49)   City or well water.

(50)   Through (54) List the closest school, its street address or distance from your house and the grades it includes.

(55)   List any parochial, private or special schools, or other colleges.

(56)   List the closest shopping center, approximate how many stores it has and list the closest large shopping center, approximate its stores.

(57)   Where is the nearest bus stop, train station for commuters, etc.?

(58)   List a number of churches by denomination.

(59)   Distance to the nearest major hospital.

(60) through (62)   Distance to these facilities.

(63)   How far to a major freeway, to a large business complex, a manufacturing plant, the downtown area, a

golf course, the seashore, a lake or other important places of interest.

(64) and (65)   Who delivers these in your area?

(66)   List the newspapers normally delivered in your area.

(67)   Self explanatory.

So, get busy and fill out this valuable *Fact Sheet* using the first empty set as your work sheet. Once you have all the information correct recopy on the final sheets. Make copies of your completed forms to give to your sincere prospects.

Now we've finally reached the point where we can establish a price, so read on.

Sample   **FACT SHEET—ONE**

Address: _____ County: _____

City: _____ State: _____ Zip: _____

Square Footage: _____ Lot Size: _____

No. Bedrooms: _____ No. Baths: _____ Age of House: _____

_____ Car Garage: _____ Basement: _____

Other Rooms: _____

_____

Major Improvements Added: _____

_____

_____

Special Features: _____

_____

_____

Items Included in Purchase Price: _____

_____

_____

Legal Description: _____

_____

_____

Zoning/Building Restrictions: _____

_____

Selling Price: _____

Terms: _____

_____

Owners: _____ Tel.: Home: _____

                                Bus.: _____

Fig. 3-1

FACT SHEET—TWO

Sample

Total Rooms: _____

Room Dimensions:

    Kitchen: _____   Bedroom: _____

    Dining Room: _____   Bedroom: _____

    Living Room: _____   Bedroom: _____

    Family Room: _____   Bedroom: _____

Financial Information:

Current Mortgage(s): _____

_____

Monthly Mortgage Payments: _____

_____

Taxes Per Year: _____   Insurance Per Year: _____

Utilities—Average Per Month:

Electricity: _____Fuel: _____   Gas: _____

Trash: _____   Water: _____   Other: _____

General Data:

Air Conditioning: _____   Heating: _____

Antenna: _____   Hot Water Tank: _____

Appliances: _____   Insulation: _____

    Elec.: _____   Landscaping: _____

    Gas: _____   Lawn Sprinklers: _____

Built-ins: _____   Patio: _____

_____   Plumbing: _____

Carpeting: _____   Roofing: _____

Drapes: _____   Sewer: _____

Elec. System (Cap.): _____   Walls: _____

    220 V Avail.: _____   Water: _____

Exterior Const.: _____

Fencing: _____

Fireplace: _____

FACT SHEET—THREE

Sample

Schools·

Elementary—Name: _____ Location: _____ Grades: ___

Secondary—Name: _____ Location: _____ Grades: ___

High School—Name: _____ Location: _____ Grades: ___

Jr. College—Name: _____ Location: _____

4-Yr. College—Name: _____ Location: _____

_____

_____

Shopping Centers: _____

_____

Public Transportation: _____

Facilities:

Churches: _____

Hospital(s): _____

Fire Station: _____ Police Station: _____

Post Office: _____

Distances to Important Points:

_____

_____

_____

Deliveries:

Bottled Water: _____ Milk: _____

Newspapers: _____

Trash Pickup: _____ times per week.

FACT SHEET—ONE

Sample

Address: _____ County: _____

City: _____ State: _____ Zip: _____

Square Footage: _____ Lot Size: _____

No. Bedrooms: _____ No. Baths: _____ Age of House: _____

_____ Car Garage: _____ Basement: _____

Other Rooms: _____

_____

Major Improvements Added: _____

_____

_____

Special Features: _____

_____

_____

Items Included in Purchase Price: _____

_____

_____

Legal Description: _____

_____

_____

Zoning/Building Restrictions: _____

_____

Selling Price: _____

Terms: _____

_____

Owners: _____ Tel.: Home: _____

                                                            Bus.: _____

FACT SHEET—TWO

Sample

Total Rooms: _____

Room Dimensions:

   Kitchen: _____   Bedroom: _____

   Dining Room: _____   Bedroom: _____

   Living Room: _____   Bedroom: _____

   Family Room: _____   Bedroom: _____

Financial Information:

Current Mortgage(s): _____

_____

Monthly Mortgage Payments: _____

_____

Taxes Per Year: _____   Insurance Per Year: _____

Utilities—Average Per Month:

Electricity: _____Fuel: _____   Gas: _____

Trash: _____   Water: _____   Other: _____

General Data:

Air Conditioning: _____   Heating: _____

Antenna: _____   Hot Water Tank: _____

Appliances: _____   Insulation: _____

   Elec.: _____   Landscaping: _____

   Gas: _____   Lawn Sprinklers: _____

Built-ins: _____   Patio: _____

_____   Plumbing: _____

Carpeting: _____   Roofing: _____

Drapes: _____   Sewer: _____

Elec. System (Cap.): _____   Walls: _____

   220 V Avail.: _____   Water: _____

Exterior Const.: _____

Fencing: _____

Fireplace: _____

FACT SHEET—THREE

Sample

Schools:

Elementary—Name: _____ Location: _____ Grades: __

Secondary—Name: _____ Location: _____ Grades: __

High School—Name: _____ Location: _____ Grades: __

Jr. College—Name: _____ Location: _____ __

4-Yr. College—Name: _____ Location: _____

_____

_____

Shopping Centers: _____

_____

Public Transportation: _____
Facilities:

Churches: _____

Hospital(s): _____

Fire Station: _____ Police Station: _____

Post Office: _____

Distances to Important Points:

_____

_____

_____

Deliveries:

Bottled Water: _____ Milk: _____

Newspapers: _____

Trash Pickup: _____ times per week.

How Is Price Established?

You have a number of basic methods available to help you establish the right price for your house. They are:

1. Make a comparison analysis of similar homes sold recently in your area.
2. Talk to realtors and brokers and get their help in setting a price.
3. Hire a professional appraiser.

Each of these will be taken up in some detail in this chapter.

COMPARISON ANALYSIS

The basic and most commonly used method in some areas to establish a market price for a house is the *Comparison Analysis*. This method compares recent sales in your neighborhood of houses of similar size and construction to yours. The basic comparison is on $ value per square foot of living area. For example, if a 1600 square foot house in your area recently sold for $64,000, that's a market value of $64,000 divided by 1600 square feet of $40 per square foot.

This $ per square foot will vary depending on the size of the lot, the condition of the house, the extras included, and all other information included in your fact sheet. Even so, it's remarkably close for a given neighborhood and type of house.

To illustrate this method, I've included figure 3-2 showing the pertinent information on the prorated sales of 39 houses in one year in a California coastal city. This is a total of $3,500,000 worth of real estate, that comes to over $200,000 in real estate commissions.

The houses listed in figure 3-2 are all in the same residential area and range in selling price from $76,000 to $127,000. The smallest house has 1300 square feet with 3 bedrooms. The largest was a 4 bedroom house with 2100 square feet.

COMPARATIVE SALES

House No.	Square Footage	Bdroms.	Extras	Listed Price (Dollars)	Selling Price (Dollars)
1	1600	3	Family Room	89,000	86,000
2	1810	4	View	99,900	95,000
3	1800	3		89,400	89,400
4	1370	3		81,990	81,990
5	1500	3		85,000	78,000
6	1390	3		83,800	80,000
7	1650	4		89,000	87,000
8	1650	4	Pool	97,000	95,000
9	1370	3		81,900	80,000
10	1800	4		93,800	90,000
11	1700	3	View	90,000	90,000
12	1700	4		91,000	90,000
13	1650	4		95,800	94,500
14	1390	3		81,900	80,000
15	2000	3	Pool	105,800	104,000
16	1990	5		97,800	94,000
17	1620	3	View & Pool	98,000	92,000
18	1390	3		91,000	88,600
19	1440	3		85,800	82,000
20	1450	3		87,900	85,000
21	1400	3		79,800	76,000
22	1930	4	View & pool	105,800	104,500
23	1630	3		93,800	93,800
24	2100	4	View & Pool	129,900	127,000
25	1440	3		85,800	82,000
26	1300	3		97,600	87,000
27	1650	4	View	93,800	93,000
28	1300	3		85,800	83,400
29	1490	3		87,900	85,000
30	1390	3		87,000	84,000
31	1980	3		105,000	102,000
32	1650	4	View	95,000	94,000
33	1660	3	View	103,000	99,800
34	1630	3		103,800	101,800
35	1540	3	View	105,800	103,800
36	1650	4		97,900	97,000
37	1400	3		95,900	93,000
38	1390	3	View	89,800	88,000
39	1390	3		93,900	92,000

Figure 3-2

Selling Dollars per sq. ft.	Month Listed	Month Sold	Days to Sell	Dollars below asking price	Percent below asking price
54	Nov	Feb	105	3,000	3.5
52	Feb	Feb	3	4,900	5
50	Feb	Feb	4	0	0
60	Feb	Feb	3	0	0
52	Dec	Mar	103	7,000	9
58	Dec	Mar	90	3,800	4.8
53	Jan	Mar	46	2,000	2.3
58	Feb	Mar	18	2,000	2
58	Mar	Mar	3	1,900	2.4
50	Mar	Apr	22	3,800	4.2
53	Apr	Apr	6	0	0
53	Apr	Apr	5	1,000	1
57	Apr	May	16	1,300	1.4
58	Apr	May	20	1,900	2.4
52	Apr	May	17	1,800	1.7
47	Apr	June	63	3,800	4
57	Mar	Jul	126	6,000	6.5
64	May	Jul	52	2,400	2.7
57	May	Jul	40	3,800	4.6
59	Jun	Jul	27	2,900	3.4
54	Jun	Jul	25	3,800	5
54	Jun	Jul	5	800	1
58	Jun	Jul	6	0	0
60	Jun	Jul	13	2,900	2.3
57	Jun	Jul	40	3,800	4.6
67	Jun	Jul	27	10,600	12
56	Jul	Jul	10	800	1
64	Jul	Jul	11	2,400	2.9
57	Jun	Aug	55	2,900	3.4
60	Jul	Sept	61	3,000	3.6
52	Aug	Sept	26	3,000	2.9
57	Aug	Sept	20	1,000	1
60	Sept	Sept	1	3,200	3.2
62	Sept	Oct	6	2,000	2
67	Sept	Oct	13	2,000	2
59	Oct	Oct	15	2,900	1
66	Oct	Oct	17	2,900	3
63	Oct	Nov	5	1,800	2
66	Nov	Nov	6	1,900	2

The price per square foot ranges from $47 to $67. This figure is somewhat misleading, however, because the price of the lot and the extras (pool, etc.) are included in this figure. Still, this data does show certain trends.

Note that the price per square foot is higher for the smaller (less than 1600 square foot) houses (typically $60 per square foot). You're paying this price to live in a specific location. A large house has a lower figure, typically $52 per square foot. A pool and a view do not add much to the price per square foot.

The average house in this list of 39 homes has about 1600 square feet and sold for about $91,000. The average time to sell a house was 29 days. The average house sold for $2640 less than the asking price, which is three percent below the asked price.

The average 3 bedroom house sold in 33 days, the average 4 bedroom in less than half that time, 16 days. 4 bedrooms are generally more sought after.

The average house, having more than 1600 square feet of living area, sold in 20 days, in only 2/3 of the time required for the average of all houses to sell.

The average house with a pool (I discarded House 17 because it's way off the average and because of the small sample of homes with pools) sold in 13 days. A house with a pool is likely to sell faster, but the owner won't get back the money he invested in the pool. About $56 per square foot was realized with houses with pools, slightly less than the average $57 for all houses.

The average house with a view sold in under 10 days (again discarding House 17), about 1/3 the average for all houses. Here again the view helped the owner sell faster, but the owner realized only a little higher priced value per square foot, or about $58.

One conclusion from the above data is that if your house has something different from your neighbors such as a larger yard, pool, a view, a modernized kitchen, an elegant bathroom, etc. you will probably sell faster (if your price is reasonable), but you won't get your investment back for your extras. The price for your house is pretty much locked in to the going price per square foot for your neighborhood.

Homes which sold in 10 days or less came down an average of only $1400. Notice that Houses 3, 4, 11 and 23 sold in 6 days or less and the seller got the listed price. If a seller receives an offer in the first few days, this first offer will likely be the best one.

When we sold our house we received an offer to buy at our listed price in a week. Unfortunately the couple couldn't qualify financially for a loan, but it was still the best of all the offers we recieved for our house.

Of course there is no way of knowing how many offers the sellers of these 39 homes turned down before they sold, but generally the longer the house was on the market, the more the seller had to cut the price. In figure 3-2 you'll note that houses on the market for over 60 days came down an average of over $4,400, or more than 5 percent.

The most any seller came down in price was 12 percent, but this house was obviously overpriced in the beginning. Even so this seller (House 26) received one of the highest prices per square foot ($66), and the house was sold in less than a month.

It's also interesting to note the months in which the houses were sold as summarized in the table below, figure 3-3.

NUMBER OF HOUSES SOLD PER MONTH

JANUARY	0	JULY	12
FEBRUARY	4	AUGUST	1
MARCH	5	SEPTEMBER	4
APRIL	3	OCTOBER	4
MAY	3	NOVEMBER	2
JUNE	1	DECEMBER	0

Figure 3-3

As one would suspect, December and January are good months for real-estate people to take a vacation, not only in sunny California, but also in wintry Maine.

July is the best month to sell, and 6 of the 12 houses sold in July were bought within a few days of the Fourth of July. This July figure probably reflects the trends of the house-buying-public with children. They'll spend the month of June looking, then buy in July so they'll have time to get their house through escrow and move in by late August or September, before school starts.

So, if you can pick the month in which to sell your house, start advertising near the first of June and count on selling in July. We started advertising our house in the latter part of June and sold our house on July 16.

TALK TO REALTORS AND BROKERS

Realtors and brokers, since it's usually their full–time occupation, keep on top of the current market prices for homes. You can take advantage of their specialized know–how by inviting a few realtors in to look over your home and to give you an estimate of what they think it will sell for. If any balk at helping you, remember they have plenty of competition in their field.

Level with the realtors, tell them you're going to try to sell your house by yourself for about a month. Then if you don't sell it you'll hire one of them. But don't make any tentative selection nor commitment to any realtor at this time.

Call the realtors in to look at your house after you've finished fixing up and your house is in a ready-to-show condition. Invite only one realtor over at a time. And make sure the realtors are actively selling homes in *your* area since property values vary considerably from one section of the city to another, from one housing area to a nearby, different housing area.

The realtor should give you a comparison chart similar to that shown in figure 3-4. By using houses of similar size and construction, the realtor will prepare this type of chart based on houses sold in recent weeks.

Realtor's Comparison Analysis
HOUSES FOR SALE

	Bedrooms	Baths	Listed Price	Square Footage	Dollars per sq. ft.	
A	4	1¾	$113,800	1,650	69	
B	4	1½	$109,000	1,650	66	
				(Average)	67.5	

HOUSES RECENTLY SOLD

	Bedrooms	Baths	Listed Price	Square Footage	Dollars per sq. ft.	Month Sold
C	4	1½	$103,000	1,650	62	April
D	3	1¾	$105,000	1,650	64	May
E	3	1¾	$109,000	1,650	66	June
F	3	1¾	$106,000	1,650	64	June
				(Average)	64	

Figure 3-4

The average listing price was about $68 per square foot, the average selling price was $64 per square foot. This turned out to be excellent information because I listed my house for $66 per square foot and sold my house for $64 per square foot.

A word of caution, however. This analysis must be done by an honest, sincere realtor. Most realtors are honest, but, like all professions, a small percentage may not be trustworthy. That's why you should insist on a written comparison analysis as shown in figure 3-4. And get more than one analysis to see how the realtors compare. Don't take anyone's word for what they say they can get for your house.

One type of realtor will inflate the value of your house, just to get you to agree to sell with that particular company. The other type will *lowball* you, quote you a low price. Steer clear of these types of realtors.

If you insist that each of the 3 to 5 realtors who inspect your house give you a written comparison analysis similar to figure 3-4, you can rely on this information.

From this data you can easily calculate a price per square foot at which you can list your property. Take an average of what the realtors estimate. If one of their estimates is way out of line, discard it. If they've done a sincere job, all of the estimates should be pretty close.

Advertise your house at a price based on the listed price per square foot ($66 per square foot in my case), but be prepared to negotiate down to the selling price per square foot ($64 in my case).

HIRE A PROFESSIONAL APPRAISER

You can hire a skilled professional to appraise the value of your house. They'll charge from $2 to $4 per $1,000 value of your house. On a $50,000 house, the professional appraiser will charge $100 to $200. This fee is tax-deductible from profits you make on your house.

To locate an appraiser, check your telephone directory, or you can call the county courthouse. They should have a list of people appointed as appraisers in the county and those who specifically work in your area, along with the appraisers' fee schedules.

A prospective buyer may insist on an appraisal, or you may wish to invest the money to see how close the other methods come to establishing a *right* price for your house, or you may have trouble obtaining enough data for a comparison analysis.

Remember, setting the *right* price is one of the most

important steps in selling a house, so put forth your best efforts on this step.

If you hire an appraiser, be sure you select a professional who belongs to a national organization, such as the *American Institute of Real Estate Appraisers.*

If you want to consider selling your house to a VA or FHA qualified buyer, you can get a VA or FHA appraisal for around $50. VA and FHA appraisers are booked up a long time ahead, so arrange early if you need their appraisal.

Selling your house under a VA or FHA loan has its disadvantages because *points* are charged in making such loans (See page 113). Since the law forbids the buyer from paying points, you, the seller, must pay these points.

For appraisals in general, no matter how expert, your appraiser can still only give you a ballpark estimate. For example, when the appraiser from the mortgage company came out to appraise our house, he asked my wife what we sold it for, then made a note on his pad. And, surprise! My house came out appraised at that *precise* value.

If you're selling your house at or below the appraised price, show this appraisal to the buyer. It's another good selling point.

Make Your Own Comparison Analysis

Now it's time for you to make your own comparison analysis. You can't expect to get as much information as I did in figure 3-2, but you should get comparative data for from 5 to 10 houses in your area.

One source of this information is the real estate ads in your local newspaper. These ads list the price and the square footage of the house they're offering for sale. If this information isn't included in the ad, don't be afraid to phone the seller, or realtor, and ask for this data. And,

visit as many of these houses and check to see if they're
in about the same condition as yours. But, remember
these ads will give you the *listed* price per square foot.

Many local newspapers list the real estate transactions
for the week as reported by the County Clerk. This listing often includes the buyer's and seller's names, the
legal description of the property, plus the selling price,
and square footage. Keep a note of the transactions in
your area. These will provide actual selling dollars per
square foot.

Ask your friends and neighbors about any of the
houses which have sold in your neighborhood recently.
Note this information, but use it with caution. Some people will conceal what they sold their house for, even
though the selling price is a matter of public record. Just
go visit the County Clerk's office and you can get the actual selling price.

Another possible source is to talk to your bank or
mortgage company. They'll often give you an idea of
how much they'd loan you on your house.

Drive around your neighborhood and visit all of the
homes which are for sale, whether by owner or through a
realtor. It pays to know your competition. At each of
these homes record the pertinent data such as price,
square footage, number of bedrooms, general condition,
etc. Again, keep in mind these are listing prices.

CHECK COUNTY CLERK'S OFFICE

You can find out what many similar homes in your area
actually sold for recently by checking the real estate deeds recorded in your County Courthouse. These records
are available for public inspection.

You'll have to know the name of either the seller or
buyer and the approximate date of the transfer of title.
But armed with these you can locate this important data
in the County Clerk's office.

Collect data on 5 to 10 similar homes. Reject any sales

which are not normal. The more data you collect on houses in your area which have approximately the square footage of your house, the more accurate your estimate will be.

SET YOUR PRICE PER SQUARE FOOT

I listed 3 possible methods of establishing your price per square foot. I recommend that you use at least 2 of these techniques as cross-checks. Take the average of the 2 or 3 methods you used. They should be pretty close together or you've done something wrong, or gotten some bad information.

If you've established, for example, an average selling price of $42 per square foot from your comparison analysis and an average selling price of $44 from your talks with realtors, average these out. $42 plus $44 divided by 2 equals $43 per square foot. If your house is 1600 square feet, you intend to sell for no less than 1600 times $43 or $68,800. But this is your *minimum* price. How much room should you leave for bargaining? At what price should you list your house?

SET YOUR LISTING PRICE

I'd recommend leaving about 5 percent margin for bargaining. By studying past listing and selling prices, you may wish to leave a little more margin, if that's the custom of the area in which you live. Some areas use about 10 percent.

Your chance of some buyer meeting your listing price is about 1 in 10. You may be lucky and catch somebody who has to buy in a hurry and isn't too cost conscious, but don't count on it.

Assume yours is an average house and you're going to sell it for an average price, in an average amount of time.

In the previous example we assumed a $68,800 minimum price for your home. Adding a 5 percent margin adds $3440 to your listing price, for a new total of

$72,240. This should be rounded off upwards, say to $73,000. So, there you have it. You list your house for sale for $73,000.

4
ADVERTISE EFFECTIVELY

Now that your house is almost fixed up and ready to show, and now that you've settled on your listing price, your next step is to concentrate on attracting customers.

But you only want to attract geniuine, potential customers, not the *Sunday lookers,* the *browsers* or the nosy people. The lookers not only waste your time, they're often negative people and discouraging to deal with. You think they're interested and make a sincere effort to show them the best features of your house, but they don't even react, don't ask any questions.

So, try to concentrate all of your time and efforts with genuine, sincere prospects. For this reason, I recommend you show your house by appointment only. *Shown By Appointment Only* will not discourage a sincere buyer. Purchasing a house is a serious business and if a person takes the time to make an appointment, it's worth spending your time to show that person through your home.

You have a number of possible ways of attracting customers, they are:

1. Newspaper classified ads
2. *For Sale By Owner* signs
3. Miscellaneous, such as word-of-mouth, bulletin boards, company newspapers, etc.

NEWSPAPER CLASSIFIED ADS

One of your most powerful means of attracting potential buyers is through a newspaper classified ad. The rates are reasonable and you reach a large audience.

An estimated 1/3 of all home sales are initiated through newspaper ads. Another interesting fact revealed by a *New York Times* survey showed that *private* ads get 4 times more response than *brokers'* ads from the same space. As a private seller, this message reaches your largest possible buying public.

Before you start to write your own ad, study the real estate ads in your local and metropolitan newspapers. Skim down the columns and note which ads you stopped and read fully. Why did you stop at those specific ads? Did a key word or phrase grab your attention? Make a note of it, you may want to use that phrase in your own ad. That's precisely what you want to do in your ad, make it stand out, entice your prospects into reading your entire ad. If they don't, they won't even get to the phone number to call for an appointment.

In general, a real estate ad should include, as the minimum information, the location (some newspaper ads segregrate ads by location), type of house (e.g. ranch style, Colonial, etc.), number of bedrooms, square footage, price, and your phone number.

How To Write An Ad

A basic writing formula, discussed in Walter Campbell's excellent book, *Writing Non-Fiction*, lists the 4 essential parts of good copy. That formula, asily applied to real estate ads is:

1. *HEY!*
2. *YOU!*
3. *SEE?*
4. *SO!*

HEY! gets the reader's attention. YOU! convinces the reader that what the ad says concerns *him* or *her* *specifically*. SEE? shows the reader the important points you wish to make about your house. SO! encourages the reader to take action, in this case to call the number you've listed to make an appointment.

Let's go through and illustrate these steps, one by one, and see how they apply directly to an ad.

HEY!

Some realtors claim that the 3 most important factors which affect the value and sale of a house are location, location, and location. So, the first piece of information which a prospective customer probably looks for is the location in which you live.

Some newspapers segregrate housing ads by location, by the community or section of the city you live in, so this job may already be done for you. If your newspaper just names your general area and you want to localize it a little more, make the first, attention-getting word(s) of your ad the location, e.g., *Annandale,* or *Larchmont,* or *Palos Verdes.*

The next few attention-getting words are perhaps your most important part of your message. Here you hook your customer into reading the rest of your ad. For the next words I recommend *By Owner—Save Broker's Commission.* You don't have to tag the words *For Sale* on the beginning of this phrase because that's assumed. But the *By Owner—Save Broker's Commission* will assault your readers' eyes and minds and entice them to read further.

Again a word of caution. Since real estate salespeople spend a lot of money in advertising, some newspapers will *refuse* to print the phrase *Save Broker's Commission.* One suburban newspaper refused to print those words in my ad. Talk about freedom of the press!

If any newspaper refuses to let you print that phrase, the next best one is *By Owner—Save $s.* That will get your message across. Few home buyers can resist a genuine bargain.

YOU!

Now that you have the reader's attention, your next task is to convince the prospect that your house is *the* house for him and/or her. Pick out the 1 or 2 unique features of either your house or your location which the reader is looking for.

Just think back when you first bought your house. What was the main reason? Did you buy to be near good schools? (We did). Did you buy to be near an industrial complex where you work? Did you buy to be near the country club? Did you buy because the house has 6 bedrooms and you have 8 children? Did you buy because you wanted to live in a quiet neighborhood?

Your most likely prospects will be a couple (or individual) just like you were when you first bought your house. Slant your ad to appeal to this type of customer.

If many children live in your neighborhood and you live near good schools, state that. If you have a view of the ocean or the city, state that. If you live in a prestige area, use that selling point. If you have an extra large house, emphasize that feature.

In some sections of the country styles of houses vary considerably. Where this is important in the choice of a house, list the style, such as ranch, split level, colonial, New England, etc., in this part of your ad.

If you have a particularly attractive loan which a buyer can take over (e.g. low interest rate or low equity) this may be one of your major selling points.

Another type of customer you should aim for are people who are already living in your area buying or renting a house. As their family size changes they may want a larger or smaller house or one in a slightly different location. I'd estimate that about 20 percent of our prospective customers already lived in our area.

So, make the second part of your ad narrow your audience down to the right group, using such key-words as *walk to schools, near golf course, one acre along stream, near shopping ranch style, quiet neighborhood, 6 bedrooms, colonial style, large house, minutes to beach, prestige living, near university, custom home, 6 percent loan, low equity.*

I personally believe messages such as *owner anxious, must sell,* etc. sound like words of desparation and will bring the bargain hunters descending on you like vultures and they'll bid far below your listing price.

SEE?

Vital information to put in next are the number of bedrooms, the square footage, and the price. You might want to add 1 or 2 special features in this part of the ad, too, to further whet your buyer's appetite. For example, if you have a formal dining room, a pool, a recreation room in the basement, state that.

If your house is in good condition and clean, don't be afraid to use the word *immaculate.* The first house we sold was very clean in spite of the fact that we had 4 small kids at the time. We advertised our house as *immaculate.* Our house was sold on the very first day we put it on the market to the very first customer who walked through the house.

Other good words to put here, as applicable, are *cul-de-sac* (of great appeal to people with small children), *laundry room, pool, wet bar, low taxes, 2 yrs. old, large kitchen, new carpets, large den.* And you should list the square footage and price. Most of the calls we got about our house asked those 2 questions first because I'd made the mistake of not including that vital information in our original ad. As soon as we told the callers those facts a number of them immediately lost their interest. Our house was too small, too big, cost too much, or too little. This wasted our callers as well as our own time, so I quickly rewrote the ad to include this vital data.

Don't use expressions like *Low 60's* when you state your price. A buyer who sees this is going to pounce on you and expect to bargain you down to the 50's. State the exact price you want to sell your house for.

so!

The last part of your ad is a call to action. A typical ending is *By Appointment Only 254-0091.*

Another good action line is *Move Right In—Call For App't 392-1492.*

Or, if your house is particularly attractive outside, recently painted, and your landscaping neatly manicured, list your address and phone number as follows *By Appointment Only 2358 Birchwood Drive Tel. 254-0974.*

Listing the address lets people drive by before they make an appointment. If they like what they see, they'll phone for an appointment. If not, you'll never hear from them. That saves your time and shields you from undue discouragement.

Some people recommend you also put the words *Principals Only* in your ad which is supposed to discourage brokers from bugging you, volunteering to sell your house. But I doubt if aggressive brokers will let that phrase stop them from calling you.

WHERE, WHEN AND HOW MUCH TO ADVERTISE

Most people look at houses on weekends so, as a minimum, advertise in the Friday, Saturday and Sunday editions of the newspapers. This is also when most of your competition advertises, thus your ad will be sandwiched between a lot of other ads. So I'd recommend that you consider advertising during the week also when your ad has a better chance of standing out and attracting people's attention.

I have no statistics on how many people have bought houses as a result of weekend or weekday ads, but I know that we got a lot of calls during the week since we ran our ads all week.

Remember it takes only one interested person to buy your house so, if your budget permits it, advertise during the week, especially if you're in a hurry to sell your house. The added cost for the extra 4 days of advertising is very little, weekend advertising is the most expensive.

Which newspapers should you advertise in? That depends on where you live. I lived in a suburb of Los Angeles and advertised in both the *Los Angeles Times* (the largest metropolitan newspaper) and in one of the local suburban newspapers.

In a situation such as this you *must* advertise in both types of papers. People from out of town or living in another section of the city may not even know of the existence of the suburban papers. And some buyers concentrate their house–hunting on using the local, suburban papers.

The big dailies often reach millions of people so their ads naturally cost more. The smaller papers may serve only tens of thousands, their rates are much lower and they reach the specialized audience you're aiming at and are not as full of real estate ads as the large papers, thus making your prospect's search easier.

As for our experience, I'd judge about 60 percent of our calls came from people who read our ad in the *Los Angeles Times*, about 40 percent from people who read the local paper. It definitely pays to advertise in both.

How Much Will Advertising Cost?

First, call the classified section of each newspaper and obtain their rates, or the papers may print their rates in their daily classified section.

Some papers charge by the word. A small, local paper may, for example, allow a 15-word-minimum ad and charge 25¢ per word for an ad to run 3 days, and only 32¢ a word for a 7 day ad. (The extra 4 days is an excellent bargain.) If they charge by the word, don't abbreviate—use long, eye-catching words.

Other papers charge by the column inch. A column inch is a standard width column, one inch in height. One small paper I priced charged only $3.00 per day per column inch. You can get a lot of words in an inch of column. Get a ruler out and measure some of the ads to check this. If you buy an inch or more of column, you can also use large, bold-faced type to draw attention to your ad.

Major newspapers usually charge you by the line. They probably require a 2-line minimum and a line is limited to a specific number of characters, 32 and 33 are typical. Spaces and punctuation are included in this number of characters so you may want to use a few abbreviations.

But don't overdo it. Use abbreviations sparingly. It's very annoying to turn a clear, well–worded ad into a puzzle, just to save a few pennies.

A typical line rate for a large newspaper is $2.20 per line for a one day ad. This scales down to $1.70 per line per day for a 7 day run. That's about $36 per week for a 3 line ad, or $20 for a 3 day, 3 line ad. Some papers have lower rates if you pay cash or use a credit card, thus saving them the cost and bother of billing you later.

You can use some special gimmicks to attract the attention of your prospective customers. For example, if you can't get your first line to come out to exactly the required 33 spaces, stick one or more stars at the left corner of your ad to make your ad stand out.

Still, my favorite attention grabber takes only 8 spaces, it's 'Save $'s'.

I recommend you use at least a 3 line ad in the large metropolitan paper (2 line ads fall down and get lost at the bottom of the column) and run it on all 7 days of the week. If you run these ads in your local and metropolitan papers it'll cost about a hundred dollars for a month's good advertising coverage. This cost is tax deductible from your profits.

Let's Compose An Ad

Assume you have a 3 bedroom house and live in a suburb near schools. Your ad might look something like this:

(HEY!) ****By Owner—Save $'s***—(YOU!) *Near Schools* (33 characters)

(SEE?) *3 Bedroom—Immaculate—1520 sq. ft.* (32 characters)

(SEE?) *$72,000*—(SO!) *Appointment Only 345-2291* (33 characters)

Or, if your newspaper doesn't segregate house ads by location, consider something like this:

(HEY!) **Falls Church—By Owner—Save $* (YOU!) *Near*

(YOU!) *Barker Country Club*(SEE?) *2 Story Brick*

(SEE?) *2000 Sq. Ft. $88,000*—(SO!) *Phone 329-6841*

Practice writing a few ads until you get one you're satisfied with. And if your published ad is not bringing in the right results, change the wording. Keep changing it every week, if you have to, until you sell.

For Sale By Owner Signs

Don't sell this inexpensive and highly effective method of advertising short. I believe that about 30 to 40 percent of the people we showed through our house did so as a result of the *For Sale By Owner* sign I'd planted on our front lawn.

Many people looking for houses to buy first decide on the location they want to live in, then they drive around the neighborhood looking for just such a sign or an *Open House* sign. A large number of houses are sold as a result of people driving by and responding to the sign on the front lawn.

First of all, don't economize here. You can buy an attractive, large (about 2 feet by 3 feet) plastic sign, with the words *For Sale By Owner* professionally printed in giant letters on the sign, for a dollar or two. The sign should look like the figure below:

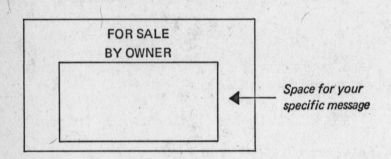

The letters should be large and easily read. Our sign had large, red letters on a black background. Since the sign was of flexible plastic, I cut out a piece of plywood and glued the sign to that strong backing, nailed a stake to the plywood, and planted the sign near the front of our yard.

The sign should have a large blank space, about 1/2 of the sign's front area, for printing your specialized message. Print the letters large so they can be easily read from the street. To make sure, walk out to the opposite side of your street and see if a person could read the message and write your phone number down without getting out of their car.

The message has to be short, so I'd suggest something like the following:

4 Bedrooms–View
By App't 345-2291

or

2000 Square Feet
By App't 562-1980

Your message is a brief commercial and gives your phone number for an appointment.

However, even if you have the words *By App't* some people won't bother to phone ahead for an appointment. They'll just drop in, say they were in the neighborhood and would like to see your house. We never turned anyone away because we figured if they were interested enough to come up and ask to see it, they were a good enough prospect to show through. One of the couples who drove by our house on the very first day we put our sign out came in without an appointment, returned a number of times to revisit our house and eventually made us a good offer 3 weeks later. You can't predict from whence your buyer will come. Use all the advertising means available to you.

Be sure you buy more than one of these signs. We put one on our front lawn, then put up a similar sign at the side of a main thoroughfare a few blocks away. The second sign, facing the traffic, should also give a short commercial and direct them to your house, for example:

4 Bedroom–Pool
27964 Wood Dr.
Right–3 Blocks

Another word of caution. Some brokers, when they see this sign, *For Sale By Owner* literally and figuratively *see red*. We had our boulevard sign torn down *three times*. One time it was stolen and we never saw it again.

I don't think a juvenile prankster was responsible. I believe a childish, irresponsible broker was. Still, that's no problem, the signs are cheap, and tax deductible from your profits, so just go out and buy another one or two.

If your second sign is placed on a wide thoroughfare, you'll have to put up 2 of them, one facing each direction of oncoming traffic.

ADVERTISING

When you're getting ready to sell your home, tell your

neighbors, your pastor, your barber, your beautician, and especially your co-workers. These people often know of new people coming into town, or of people looking for a larger or better located house.

Another way to advertise is to insert a small ad on the bulletin boards you usually find at your nearby shopping center, your church, or at work. Type up a few 3 by 5 cards and place them, free of charge, at these local sources of advertising.

Perhaps your company newspaper permits free ads. This is especially helpful if you work for a large company with branches in many cities. New employees just moving into town, employees being transfered from one plant to another, etc. often scan company newspapers for suitable houses to buy.

When a realtor holds an open house near you, place one of your spare *For Sale By Owner* signs with your address on it near (but not too near) the realtor's open house sign. That way you can induce that realtor's customers to also stop by your house. Incidentally, you must obtain a property owner's permission to place your sign on their property.

Some large companies keep listings of houses available to aid employees just moving into your city. Call the Personnel Department of these companies and ask if they would like one of your *Fact Sheets.* They often spend a lot of time and effort in helping their new employees relocate.

Don't be alarmed by all the information I've provided in this chapter. You certainly don't have to use all the possible methods of advertising. I've listed them all so you can use those which you feel give you the best results.

As a minimum I urge you to advertise in the metropolitan and local newspapers, and be sure to use the *For Sale By Owner* signs.

Now that you've attracted prospective buyers, let's discuss the technique of showing people through your house

5
SHOW YOUR HOUSE EFFECTIVELY

95 percent of the people who come to see your house won't like it. That means that 19 out of 20 people who go through your house will be turned off when they see it. This is true even though you've already weeded out most of the lookers through your ad, *By Appointment Only* and through your phone conversations. We showed about 60 couples through our house and received 3 legitimate offers.

A house is a very personalized possession. Buyer's needs and desires are so complex that probably no house in the world could ever completely satisfy anyone. So condition yourself to the fact that many if not most of your prospects will critize one or more features of your home. Don't take offense when they find fault because there are probably still some things even you don't like about your own house, though you've lived in it for years and have decorated and furnished it yourself.

Think back about all the houses you looked at before you bought your home, all the houses you didn't like. The people you show through your house deserve this same privilege.

How many times do people visit a house before they actually buy it? One survey showed:

For a New House—40 percent of the people made 5 or more trips before making up their minds.

For a Used House—50 percent made up their minds after only two trips.

And, how many houses did people look at before they bought? This same survey showed:

For New Houses—The buyers looked at more than 10 on the average and looked at houses for 3 months.

For Old Houses—Buyers looked at 5 on the average and looked for 2 months before buying.

This study showed that used houses are easier to sell, prospects looked at 5 houses before buying. And they made fewer trips to an old house before deciding to buy.

No matter how you've weeded out beforehand, you'll still have to deal with 2 kinds of people, the *lookers* and the *prospects*.

You'd like to handle only genuine prospects, but the lookers are much greater in number and virtually impossible to separate from the serious buyers. The lookers are people who have looked at houses for years, are really not serious about buying, probably don't even have the money to buy, but they *love* to look at houses. The lookers are the Sunday drivers who enjoy looking at houses like some people like going to art museums, or the zoo. The lookers are people who are going to move *one of these days*, but their day never seems to come. Lookers daydream about living above their financial resources and visit higher priced homes to dream a little.

You'll also get some real estate brokers masquerading as prospects spying on you, their competition. And you'll get some nosy neighbors, lookers who want to see what you're selling and for how much.

One thing you should consider is to hold an *Open House* one weekend to get most of the lookers out of the way. Try this the second weekend your house has been up for sale.

So, the first rule of *showing your house* is to be polite and kind and considerate to everyone who comes to look at your house. Think of these *lookers* as practice customers, guinea pigs you're practicing and perfecting your sales pitch on until a real buyer comes along. Be nice to everyone, you need only one buyer to sell your house.

There is also a tendency at first to regard every person who shows even the slightest interest in your house as a hot prospect. The first weekend we showed about 20 couples through, 3 couples seemed ready to buy right away. But they never showed up again. Why, we'll never know. So don't get your hopes up too high for your first, seemingly interested customers. You're liable to be hurt, disappointed and confused when they don't come back.

Shown By Appointment Only

Not only does *shown by appointment only* weed out a lot of the lookers, it also lets you live a halfway normal life in the house you're selling. It's impossible, and too much to ask of the people who live with you (especially your children) not to mess up, quit breathing and try to keep your house in a showing condition all the time. *By Appointment Only* gives you time to get ready for potential customers.

One very important fact to remember about selling houses is that first impressions are very, very important. If your house is dirty and you agree on short notice to show a prospect through you've made a bad decision. You'll probably never be able to erase the picture of the unmade beds, the dirty dishes in the sink and the messy living room from your customer's mind. Show people through your house only when it's in showing condition.

Even though you get some drop-ins who suddenly appear without an appointment, you can accomodate them. One way is to keep your living room (or family room, or one special *waiting room*) clean and neat 24 hours a day. Keep everybody out of this room. Then, if people show up unannounced, when the house is a bit messy, ask them to relax a moment in your waiting room until you can tidy up.

Or, if your house needs a lot of cleaning, be frank and tell your prospect your house is not in a showing condition. Ask them, in a polite way, to come back in 10 or 15 minutes. If they're interested, they'll come back.

The odds of selling a house which is messed up are very small. The prospect will long remember that unfavorable first impression.

We made the mistake once of showing a prospect through at 10 o'clock at night when the kids were in bed. The prospect sounded enthusiastic over the phone, but he quickly toured our house, said he loved the view, and disappeared from sight, never to be heard from again.

WHEN YOU SHOULD SHOW YOUR HOUSE

That's entirely up to you. If you're available to show during the week, during daylight hours, this is an excellent time. Then the kids are away at school, the traffic is at a minimum, the house is bright and the neighborhood quiet.

However, since most people who'll be looking at your house have jobs, you'll get most of your prospects on Saturday and Sunday, with Sunday afternoons being the busiest. Often, however, a wife may show up during the week and if she's really interested, will make another appointment and bring her husband on the weekend. This happened to us a number of times.

When we sold our house I was working full time and my wife stayed at home, so we accepted appointments pretty much at the convenience of the prospect, and my wife did the showing. When you show people through depends on your individual circumstances, but it's best to show in the daytime, when a house looks bright and cheery.

MAKING APPOINTMENTS BY PHONE

When you're house is on the market and people start responding to your ad, or to the sign on the front of your lawn, insist that all of the phone–answering during this period be done by the adults in the house. Keep your kids off the phone, ask them to discourage their friends from calling because from the time your ad appears until the time you sell your house your home phone is your business phone. (Sorry about that, kids, but selling a house is a serious business, a huge investment).

Be polite and sincere when you answer your phone. Be proud of your home. Your best sales psychology is your enthusiasm about your house, your neighborhood.

How much time should you allow for appointments? You'll check this out later when you make trial runs through your house, but if you don't have a lot of prospects to accomodate, allow a half hour. As a minimum, allow 15 minutes.

When your prospect asks for an appointment, see if they have a time preference. If not, suggest one. And suggest a specific time, such as, "I'll mark you down for 2:15," rather than saying, "Stop by around 2." You'll have to do this or some people will be late, some early and you'll end up with your prospects bunched up and it's awkward to try to show more than one prospect through your house at the same time. This also annoys a potential buyer because they've asked for a specific time and should be granted this time to see the house by themselves, at their own leisure.

Buy an appointment calendar to keep by the phone and write down your prospect's name and phone number opposite the time you've scheduled them. This helps with later follow–up and when a prospect calls back for a second appointment you'll know they're interested. You might also note on your appointment calendar whatever pertinent information you can find out about your prospect such as the number and age of kids they have, where they live now, where they work, etc. This will help you later as you escort them so you'll know what features of your house or neighborhood to emphasize.

You'll be bugged by real estate brokers who'll either masquerade as potential customers and make appointments (this happened to us about 6 times) or they'll admit they're brokers and say they want to make a *special deal* for you. In this highly competitive business of real estate they may ask you to take down your *For Sale By Owner* sign for just a few minutes so then can show a potential customer through, then say they can sell the house for you for your listing price, *plus* their commission. I personally consider such shenanigans dishonest. You can't offer your house for sale at 2 different prices. Shun such special deals, they're a waste of time.

Don't be discouraged by some people who phone, ask a few questions about your house, then make some disparaging comment like, "I wasn't expecting to pay that much!" and hang up. Some of these calls fall into the crank category. We had the price of our house in our ad and still people hung up saying they weren't prepared to pay that much. We often suspected some of these crank calls were from disgruntled brokers trying to discourage us from selling our own house.

If people call and don't make an appointment be grateful for this further weeding-out process. At least you haven't had to waste your time showing them through the house.

Keep a copy of your *Data Sheet* beside the telephone so you'll be prepared to answer most of your prospects' questions.

If your prospect phones and says, "So you're selling it for $63,000? Is that price firm?", this is no time to bargain, they haven't even seen your house yet. To reply you can say, "Yes, it's firm and I can sell it at *only* $63,000 because I'm splitting the broker's commission with you." There you are again using that magic phrase, *Save $'s*.

Answer your callers' questions simply, don't elaborate too much, don't seem overly anxious to sell on the phone. Tell them they really have to see the house to appreciate the huge living room, the view, the large, covered patio you've installed, or whatever.

Your function on the phone is to further weed out *lookers*, to sense which people are sincerely interested, answer their questions and encourage them to come out to see your home.

Some people will call just to get your address if it's not in your ad. They just want to drive by and see if they're interested. Give them your address, if they drive by and like what they see, they'll call back for an appointment. If they're not interested they've saved you the time of showing them through.

Some people are going to make appointments and then not show up. Don't let it discourage you. If they don't show, they weren't really that interested and you've saved the time of showing them through the house. We had many people make appointments and never show up.

WHAT KIND OF CALLS CAN I EXPECT?

You're going to get all kinds of calls, some from sincere customers, some I believe from people just released from mental institutions, and some from brokers who hassle on purpose.

I made a log of a few calls I received over a couple of weekends. Let me share them with you here so you'll have some idea of what you may run into. I've used false names for obvious reasons, but the conversations reported are factual. We had already had our house on the market for about 2 weeks before I started keeping this log.

Saturday, July 7

9:10   Mrs. Leonard called. She was looking for a home

for her nephew and lives nearby. She made an appointment to come by the house on Monday and gave me her phone number. (She did keep the appointment. She came by a number of times with other people to visit the house, and eventually made an offer to buy my house.)

9:50   A man with an English accent called and asked for my address. He said he lived in a nearby suburb and would drive by. We never heard from him again.

10:00   Mrs. Frascati called. She said she lived in a suburb about twenty miles away. She was deathly afraid of fog and sought my reassurance that we had only a little fog. I assured her we did. She asked for our address and said she would drive by. We never heard from her again.

10:50   Mrs. Stein of a realty company called. She asked if we were *cooperating with realtors*. My reply was that as long as I received my listing price I didn't care who sold it. She said she had a customer and would get hold of them and come by. They never showed up.

10:55   Mr. Richards called. He made an appointment for 12:00. He asked if the backyard was big enough for a pool. I assured him it was. He came by. He didn't seem too interested as he went through quickly. We never heard from Mr. Richards again.

11:12   Mr. Klaus called. He has 3 kids. He made an appointment for 11:45. He came by and liked the house, but said he would have to sell his own house in a nearby suburb first. He called back a couple of more times. He said he was still interested, but it would take some time to sell his house. He called back after we'd sold our house. He seemed genuinely disappointed that he hadn't been able to sell his house in time to buy ours.

11:35   Lt. Granson of the Air Force called. He would call back later if he could make it out. He lives in Los Angeles. He wants to move out into a suburb, he never called back.

12:00 Mr. Davis called. He asked if we had a formal dining room and copper plumbing. When we answered no to both questions, he snapped he wasn't interested and rudely hung up.

12:30 Mr. Bamburger called. He made an appointment at 1:30. He and his young wife came by. They seemed genuinely interested. Ours was the first house they'd looked at. They never called back.

1:45 Mrs. Bowstring and her sister stopped by unannounced. They saw the sign on our front lawn. We showed them through. Mrs. Bowstring later admitted that she and her 'sister' were brokers.

1:52 Mr. Duncan of a realty company called. He was interested in house with a view. Our house had a view, except it was the foggy season when we were selling. He said he wanted to get a house for a friend of his. He never showed up.

3:40 Mr. Caen called. He made an appointment for 6 p.m. He lived in a house in the neighborhood. He was renting the house and wanted to buy. He and his wife came by. They seemed to like the house. We never heard from them again.

4:20 Mr. D'Augustino stopped by unannounced. He has sold his house. He and his wife are temporarily living in an apartment. He seemed interested. He took my phone number, but never called back.

4:30 Mrs. Gonzales called to get address and directions to our house. That was the last we heard of her.

7:30 A Laurie Baskins of a realty company called. She asked us to take our *For Sale By Owner* sign down when she showed one customer through. I refused. She hung up on me.

Saturday, July 14

Starting with this date my wife and I announced to all interested people that on the following Monday we would be turning our house over to a realtor and the price of our house would go up by 6 percent, the realtor's commission. So we were holding a *weekend special*.

9:00   Mr. Denson called. He made an appointment for 2 or 3 o'clock. We should have made an appointment for a specific time. He'd called earlier in the week, but never showed up.

9:10   Mr. Fields called. He said it was too cold for a pool where we lived. Our next door neighbor and the house across the street both had pools. He said he might come and look if he was in the area. Luckily he never showed.

9:20   Mr. Donovan called. He made a 10 o'clock appointment. He wanted to know if we had a family room. We didn't. He later cancelled his appointment. He was about the only no—show who had the courtesy to phone and cancel.

10:00   Mr. Samuels called. He asked for the square footage, in spite of the fact that the square footage was in our ad. He said it was too small for him.

10:15   Mr. DeLeo made an appointment for 2:30. He showed up at 3:30. He went through house quickly. He asked no questions. He vanished forever from our lives.

11:45   Mr. Dugan of a realty company called. He offered to sell my house for me. I said I wasn't interested. I looked up his firm in the phonebook. Their ad said they specialized in beachfront property. I lived a couple of miles from the ocean. Only a huge tidal wave or an earthquake would have converted my lot into beachfront property.

12:10   An unidentified woman called. She said she'd seen our ad in the Los Angeles Times. She asked price, etc., in spite of the fact our ad listed our price. She finally said it was too expensive for her.

12:50   Mrs. Pike drove by. She saw our sign. She dropped in. She asked for the square footage. She said she was looking for something bigger and left.

1:30 Mr. Burger of a nearby suburb called. He wanted to come at 2:30, but said he may come tomorrow. He had three kids. This man later bought our house. You see it's worth putting up with all the hassle and disappointment ahead of this, just to receive this one call. At this time, however, Mr. Burger was just another prospect who'd made an appointment.

1:35 Mr. Wong called. He said he would call back after 3:30 for an appointment. He did call back later.

3:00 Mr. Burger came by. He seemed extremely interested. He asked many questions. He and his wife looked over our house carefully. They asked about the schools, etc. He said he would call back the next day.

5:00 Mr. Steppen of a realty company said he'd be by tomorrow to look at the house. He never showed.

5:10 The Wongs came to see our house. They had a house in a neighboring suburb which they had to sell first. This couple was extremely interested. I'm sure if they'd been able to sell their house in time, they would have bid on our house. They came back twice the next day to go through our house again. This was a sign of very definite interest.

Sunday, July 15

I took my kids and spent most of the day at a Kathryn Kuhlman Religious Service. I left my wife at home to escort any interested parties. She told them all the price was going up by 6 percent on the morrow.

My wife escorted perhaps a dozen new couples through the house, plus 6 couples who had been through our house one or more times before.

When I got home at 5:30 one prospect, Mr. Gabriel, was waiting, with his entire family. He had a written offer for me. Earlier in the day Mr. Leonard (who'd visited our house a week earlier) had already delivered a written offer to buy my house, but his offer was very low. And thirdly a message was waiting for me to call Mr.

Burger who had been by earlier in the day also. I called him. He made a satisfactory offer on the spot. We briefly discussed mutually agreeable terms, such as an escrow company, moving-out day, etc., and we agreed to meet at the escrow company at 10 the next morning.

Since Mr. Burger's offer was the highest and most attractive from all aspects, I verbally accepted his offer and formally rejected the offers from Mr. Gabriel and Mr. Leonard.

I met Mr. Burger at the escrow office the next morning and he was tentatively financially qualified on the spot by the loan officer. We went into escrow about 11, signed papers, and before noon that day my house was sold.

I've shared some of our personal experiences to help prepare you for what you may have to put up with in selling your own house. One of the biggest problems in making appointments by phone and showing people through your house is discouragement. A few of your prospects will be rude, inconsiderate and downright insulting. Be prepared. Don't let them offend you.

When you feel a little discouraged after dealing with some of these people just think of all that beautiful green you're going to make when that one *right* customer comes along and buys your house.

Was it worth it? Would I do it again if I had the change? I most assuredly would! All it takes is one person to buy a house. You may have to deal with 20, 50 or more personalities. But when the *right* person comes along, you'll forget all about the kooks you had to deal with. And whenever you have an impolite, rude person to escort, just thank God you don't have to live in that person's shoes.

In defense of humanity, however, let me assure you that most of the people we showed through were courteous and sincere in their interest. Even so, our house had one or more things they didn't like. Or, perhaps they didn't have the money to afford it, or in some cases they had to sell their present house before they could make an offer on ours.

Just remember there are so many reasons, so many complex, interrelated factors involved in buying a house that you shouldn't be discouraged if 19 out of 20 prospects aren't interested in your house.

Keep reminding yourself that *one* buyer is all you need.

GET READY TO SHOW

In Chapter 2 I suggested you make sure your yard and house were neat, neat, neat. You want to keep it in that condition or restore it to that condition before each prospect goes through. By now you should have the message *first impressions are lasting* engraved on your mind. Keep your front yard neat, orderly, the hoses rolled up, the lawn and shrubs clipped, the driveway clean.

Realtors say, "Half the battle of selling a house is getting the buyers out of their car." If the prospects don't like the look of your front yard it's unlikely they'll ring your doorbell and keep their appointments.

Inside the house empty all the ashtrays and wash the mirrors. Set up a vase of fresh flowers and a bowl of fresh fruit. Put clean bedspreads on the beds. Put an ironed tablecloth on the table. Turn on enough 100 watt bulbs in the house to make it light and bright.

Put new, unused bars of soap in your bathroom sink, your shower and your kitchen. Hang up your best clean towels or buy some new ones especially for this showing and take them and the soap away and save them for the next day's showing.

Dust the usual places and some of the unusual places.

Check all the closets to make sure the doors work and the closets are neat and uncluttered. Put all the dirty clothes in a closed hamper.

Make sure there are no cooking odors when you are showing. Use room deodorizer if you have the smell of bacon left over from breakfast. Or if you want to create a really favorable first impression, buy some of the ready–to–bake loaves of bread at the store and bake them. Leave them cooling in the kitchen to give off their delectable odor when your prospects arrive. There's nothing like the smell of fresh-baked bread to make someone feel *at home*. Because you're not selling a house, you're selling a *home*.

Does all this sound unnecessary or foolish? Decide that for yourself but remember that you have a lot of money riding on a successful sale. You should try hard to create a good, first impression.

Send your kids over to the neighbors or to a babysitters or to a movie. You don't need their help at a time like this. And you should also keep your pets out of sight. I've personally found it annoying to have a dog jumping all over me when I looked through a house. Send your cat out looking for a mouse and drape the night-cover on the parakeet's cage. Put some quiet background music on your radio or stereo. Turn off all the appliances such as the dishwasher or dryer. Pull the plug out on the TV set. If the weather is a little nippy, build a fire in your fireplace. A crackling fire, even gas flames on artificial logs, spells HOME to many people.

If your house and neighborhood appeal to families with children the odds are good that the parents will bring their kids with them when they look at your house. Be prepared. Set up a little table, chairs, coloring books and crayons in one of the bedrooms, perhaps even a game. Maybe one of your older children can help babysit your prospects' kids, take them outside to the swing set and keep them out of their parent's way while your prospective customers look at your house.

Be ready for one important question your prospects will ask. "Why are you selling your house?" They'll want to know why you are now aparently dissatisfied with your house.

I sold my house because I moved out of town. That's an excellent reason. Some people sell because their family is growing and they need a larger house. Some sell because their children have grown up, left home and they need a smaller house. Some people move to get closer to their jobs. All these are valid reasons. There's no need to tell them you're moving because you can't get along with your neighbor, they might become good friends with your next door neighbor.

There are probably more than one reason why you're moving. Give your prospects the one that sounds the most reasonable.

SHOWING PROSPECTS THROUGH

Who should show prospective customers through your home? That depends on your situation. My wife, since she exuded enthusiasm about our house (and since I'm a lousy salesman), showed most of the prospects through. Sometimes she was absent or busy and I had to show people through.

Both of you should be prepared to show customers through. The one who is by temperament and personality the best salesperson should do most of the showing. And make some trial runs with one mate escorting the other through the house, or use a neighbor or friend as a *guinea pig*. Time these tours. Go through your sales pitch. Test each other out by asking questions about the house.

Make yourself neat and presentable when you're getting ready to escort people. Put a tie on, a clean dress and greet your prospects warmly at the front door. Introduce yourself and get their names if you don't already have them listed on your appointment calendar. They are guests in your house, so treat them accordingly.

Don't let your customers go through your house unescorted. They'll get lost and won't be able to recognize and appreciate the features of each room unless you're with them to point them out.

Because first impressions are so lasting, start your tour in the best room in the house whether it be the modernized kitchen, the large living room, or the recreation room in the basement. If your backyard is exceptional and has a pool or beautiful landscaping start there. A good first impression will help a prospect overlook minor objections later.

Show your prospects through the house at a leisurely pace. Don't talk too much. Let them open the closets and ask questions. Listen carefully to their questions. If they start asking detailed questions like size of the hot-water tank, room sizes, etc. they're probably more than just lookers. Be prepared to show them the garage, the basement. Mention the 220 volt line you have in the basement for power tools or the built-in work bench which goes with the house.

Watch their faces as they go from room to room. Expressions often give you a truer picture than words of what they really think about your house. Enthusiasm and interest will be written on their faces, as will disinterest and boredom.

Again, keep your enthusiasm up, even though some prospects seem to delight in finding things wrong with your house.

I remember one man in particular who came through our house and kept making disparaging comments. I kept my temper as he told me, "This rug has to be replaced". The rug was only a couple of years old and in good shape. When he added, "The entire backyard will have to be redone," I clenched my fist inside my pants pocket. I'd just finished redoing the entire backyard a month earlier. He kept insulting my house, but I stayed cool.

A prospect who does this is setting you up for a low bid on your house. They think that by downgrading your house they'll convince you it's worth little and buy it cheaper. This man almost got a mouthful of bare knuckles. However he did make a bid on my house during my weekend special. As I expected, he lowballed me. His bid was a few thousand dollars below the other bid I received.

As you tour the house don't keep chattering to fill in the silence. Give your prospects time to look and think.

Mention inconspicuous details as you show them through. If a closet has a light in it, turn it on for them. If your patio is big enough for a pingpong table, mention that. Tell them about the beautiful sunsets you can see from your living room window.

Also mention other points which are not obvious to the prospect. "My dishwasher is only 6 months old", or "We just put new tile in this bathroom", etc. Don't overdo it. A constant chatter is annoying and unnerving.

MENTION THE SCHOOLS, THE NEIGHBORHOOD

Your prospect is also interested in your neighborhood. If they have kids tell them about the schools, how far they are, how close the nearest park is. If there are swimming pools in the neighborhood or a country club six blocks away, mention that. Be prepared to answer their questions about churches, shopping centers and the ages of the other children in the neighborhood which their kids would play with.

Let the prospects proceed at their own pace. Try to find out what they want, what they're looking for, good schools, a quiet neighborhood or whatever. Listen to what the wife says to her husband, and vice versa.

End your tour on a positive note. Final impressions are also lasting. End up in your second best room, your second best feature. You may end up in your living room, your patio, or the large dining room. At this point if you have not already done so, let your prospect sit down and study your *Fact Sheet*. You might want to leave the husband and wife alone now to let them talk in private.

But don't expect them to make you an offer then and there. Buying a house is much too complicated and too huge an investment to make a decision after a 15 minute tour. Chances are they'll ask a lot of questions, request a copy of your *Data Sheet* and ask for a chance to think it over. Give them a *Data Sheet* and be sure you get their name and phone number. Never let them know you're overly anxious to sell in a hurry or you put yourself at a disadvantage.

If they're really interested and don't want to leave offer them coffee. Sit down and talk. They may want to tour the house again. If they go this far they're very eager so hold on to them.

HOW TO ANSWER QUESTIONS

You *must* answer questions truthfully. But don't volunteer any information needlessly. You don't have to tell your prospect that the dishwasher is about to break down, etc.

The doctrine of *Caveat Emptor* prevails when you're selling your house. Translated to English this means *let the buyer beware*. In other words, you're selling your house in an *as is* condition and it's up to the buyer to uncover any faults or shortcomings about your house.

Be careful. You can't lie in response to any questions a prospect asks. If you knowingly lie and the person buys your house, moves in and later finds out you deliberately lied, the buyer can sue you. You cannot deliberately deceive anyone but you're not obligated to tell your prospect everything that is wrong with your house. This is a case where *silence is golden.*

Try to counter a negative question with a positive statement. If your buyer asks, "Does the clother dryer go with the house?" you could counter with, "No, but the dishwasher is included in the price."

IS THE PROSPECT GENUINELY INTERESTED?

A number of telltale signs will let you know when a prospect is genuinely interested. First you'll note an interested prospect will ask a wide variety of detailed questions ranging from the size of your house heater, to the type of plumbing you have, to the churches in your neighborhood, to the quality and type of the schools nearby. They'll ask what kind of a neighborhood you live in, what the next door neighbors are like and what kind of work they do. Answer all of their questions no matter how detailed and seemingly unimportant they are. These questions are important to the person who asked them.

But the surest sign of a serious prospect is when they make return visits or keep calling you up on the phone to ask more detailed questions. Note that in the early part of this chapter I said that 50 percent of the people who buy a used house decided to buy after only 2 trips. But many more make more than only 2 trips. We had some serious prospects who made at least 6 trips to our house. They were probably narrowing down their choice to 2 or 3 houses. They revisited and compared them repeatedly in the process of making their final decision.

So when your prospects come back, bringing their mother–in–law to show her the house, when they come back and measure the space for their refrigerator or their hi-fi, and when they try to feel you out by making verbal offers (don't accept verbal offers, see Chapter 6), then you know they're serious.

On most routine sales you'll soon get to the point where a prospect will say, "I'm interested in buying your house and I want to make you an offer."

"Fine," you'll reply, trying not to grin too widely. "If you'll put your offer in writing, I'll be glad to sit down with you and discuss it." Chapter 6 tells you how to handle this situation.

Or you may find yourself in a situation where you have more than one serious prospect, all interested, all have been back for repeat visits, or have called you many times. But you can't seem to get them to act. You may be running out of time. That's the situation I found myself in.

How do you move your prospects into action? Why not try what I did, a weekend special?

A WEEKEND SPECIAL

Once I got to the point where I had about 5 prospects seriously interested in our house, I decided it was time to urge these people into action.

On a Saturday morning we informed everyone who called for an appointment or for information that on the following Monday morning we were going to turn our house over to a realtor to sell. And on Monday morning the price would be going up by 6 percent, the realtor's commission. We informed our prospects that they could make bids up to and including Sunday night on our weekend special and save the 3 percent commission. That was a $6,000 increase in price in our case.

To sweeten the competition we told every serious person that a number of people were interested in the house and would be making bids also. The stage was set. (There were 5 serious prospects at the time).

From Saturday morning on through to Sunday night our house was on special. We were serious. We had about run out of time. I was going to quit my job and we were packing to move out of town. It was a genuine weekend special. On Monday we were going to turn it over to a realtor.

It worked. Of the 5 interested prospects we received 3 firm offers in writing. I accepted the highest offer on Sunday night and the house was sold.

So, if you get to the point of where you have a number of potential customers dangling, ready to bid, but too indecisive to do anything about it, try a weekend special.

Tell all your prospects you're seriously considering giving your house to a broker to sell on Monday and that they can bid on it for a 6 percent lower price for that weekend only. If that doesn't jar them into action they weren't really that serious about the house. So, if you lose them, you haven't lost much.

But don't try this weekend special unless you have one or more definitely serious prospects.

What happens if it doesn't work? Suppose you hold your weekend sale, and nobody bites?

That's up to you. You could delay it for a few more days, say give it another week, come Monday. After all you were only seriously considering turning your house over to a broker. Besides you can always change your mind and continue selling it yourself.

Or if you're tired of trying to sell your home, you could turn it over to a broker. Don't worry about a broker not taking it. Real estate is a highly competitive business and they'll try to sell it for you, for your listing price, plus their commission.

Now that you're ready to receive more offers, let's see how to handle them.

6
HOW TO HANDLE OFFERS

You now have one or more prospects who are definitely serious about your house. They've been back once, twice, or more times to go through your house and have asked a lot of detailed questions. They've called you on the phone a couple of times to ask other questions. You now want to transform a prospect into a purchaser.

Before you consider any offers, heed this extremely valuable advice from experienced realtors: *the first offer is usually the best offer and is usually received in the first month.* So consider your first offer very carefully.

This was precisely my personal experience, also. The first offer we received was the best offer and was made after our house had been on the market for only a few days. Unfortunately our prospects, although sincere in their desire to buy our house, were unable to qualify for a loan, so the deal fell through. But that was just bad luck.

The basic steps in considering offers are:
1. You receive a *written* offer.
2. You accept, reject or make a counter–offer.
3. You negotiate the details.
4. You and the buyer sign an *Agreement of Sale* and you accept the buyer's deposit. You must now take your house off the market, because it's sold.
5. Your buyer gets a preliminary loan committment from his lender and you and the buyer sign a *Contract of Sale of Real Estate* (or similar form).
6. You go into escrow.

We'll take the first 5 steps in this chapter. Escrow will be covered in Chapter 7.

YOU RECEIVE A WRITTEN OFFER

Some buyers' first tendency is to feel you out on price verbally. If a prospect asks, "Would you consider an

offer of around $50,000?" and you've listed your house at
$56,000 refuse to discuss verbal offers for some very
good reasons.

An offer has to be in writing, signed and dated to make
it a valid offer. It doesn't have to be notarized but it must
be in writing. Handshakes just don't stand up in court.

If you get a verbal offer and quickly reply, "Yes, I
might consider $50,000," you're letting yourself in for a
lot of trouble. The buyer will quickly sense your
overeagerness and try to bid you down even further.
Verbal comments aren't binding. When you get down to
negotiating the details of the offer, the buyer may be
completely impossible and unreasonable and try to get
you to throw your piano, washer, dryer and car in for the
$50,000.

Instead of verbally replying to such a question, tell
your prospect, "Put your offer in writing and I'll give it
serious consideration." Only when you have an offer in
writing can you see what conditions your buyer has attached. I'll illustrate this shortly with some sample offers.

Insisting on a written offer also stops a lot of the need-
less haggling from insincere lookers who are only playing a game with you on price. If they're serious they'll
put it in writing. Don't be surprised if you get one or two
low, even insultingly low offers for your house. A certain breed of people do this either out or perverse mean-
ness or in an attempt to get a real basement bargain
which they can later resell at a profit.

So don't feel insulted, just be glad you don't have to
live in that person's tennis shoes.

You Accept, Reject Or Make A Counter–offer

After a prospect has made you a written offer, you
have three choices. We'll take these up one at a time.

But, first consider the following examples of written offers, what information *might* be in them, what information *should* be in them to protect you, the seller.

July 1, 19xx

Mr. and Mrs. Arnold Jersey
    I hereby offer to purchase the property known as 2783 Corona Place, Norman, Oklahoma, for $55,000. This offer is subject to granting of a loan to cover the purchase.

Sincerely,
Eldon W. Hayes

This is a nice, short and delicious offer. Mr. Hayes will probably be fairly easy to negotiate with since he has put in only one condition, that he be granted a loan, which is a perfectly reasonable request. Generally, the less the prospect puts in a buy offer the better it is for you, the seller. As long as the prospect has put in the minimum information—the date, price, address and signed it—this offer is adequate for the moment.
    Here's another type of offer:

August 21, 19xx

Mr. James J. James
1325 Meadowlark Road
Minneapolis, Minnesota.

Dear Mr. James,
    I herewith offer to purchase from you, free and clear of all encumbrances, the real property commonly described as 1325 Meadowlark Road, Minneapolis, Minnesota, including built-ins, drapes, carpeting and affixed shelving or bookcases, all located at said premises, for the total sum of $50,000.
    This offer is considered to be valid for 3 days

and is contingent upon my obtaining proper financing.

Sincerely,
Joan Diffenderfer

Here also is a valid offer and the terms are perfectly reasonable. Joan Diffenderfer has also included a few extra conditions, such as what's included in the purchase price. But if this is what you listed on your *Fact Sheet* as going with the house your prospect has made a proper offer.

In theory the items included on your *Fact Sheet* as going with the house are valid only if the prospect meets your price listed on the *Fact Sheet,* so this leaves you room for bargaining if your prospect comes in with a lower dollar bid.

Here's another type of offer you may also unfortunately receive:

April 1, 19xx

Mr. Thomas Merton
2130 Boyle Avenue
Boston, Mass.

Dear Sir

This letter confirms my offer of $40,000 on your house located at 2130 Boyle Avenue. Mortgage is to be obtained at Northern Federal with a 10 percent downpayment, and at a 9 percent interest rate.

Sincerely,
Horatio Alpert

Mr. Alpert has just lowballed you. And, he has made his offer contingent on his getting a loan at a specific mortgage company for an interest rate lower than the prevailing rate. You're almost insulted by Horatio's offer. Turn it into a positive tool. Use it for bargaining with other prospects. If your first prospect is balking a little you can wave your other offer or offers in your buyer's face to break down your prospect's reluctance. Wave them fast so the buyer can't read them. There's nothing like competition to close a sale, to force a recalcitrant prospect to make a decision.

And now let's take a look at one written by a man who knows a little too much about real estate:

April 1, 19xx

Mr. and Mrs. Dalton A. Price, Esq.
28940 Greendell Street
Cincinnati, Ohio.

My dear Mr. and Mrs. Price,

I herewith offer to purchase from you, free and clear of all encumberances, the real property commonly described as 28940 Greendell Street, Cincinnati, Ohio, including built-ins, curtains, drapes, storm windows, screens, carpeting, TV antenna, swing set, work bench, and any affixed shelving or bookcases, all located at said premises, for the total sum of $52,000.

This offer is subject to all of the following conditions:

1. I am able to secure a loan in the principal sum of $46,800 secured by said real property payable over a period of 30 years, at an annual interest rate of not more than 10 percent, and that payment of points (See Chapter 7) be shared equally by buyer and seller.

2. You and I can mutually agree, in writing, on terms necessary to implement a proposed contract of sale, title policies, termite inspection and treatment if necessary, and other related matters, per escrow instructions.

3. An appraisal shall be performed by an appraiser of my choosing. If the appraised value is less than $52,000, this offer will be considered null and void.

4. All appliances (range, dishwasher, air conditioner, oven, water heater, furnace, etc.) shall be in working order at time of closing.

If this offer is acceptable to you, please so indicate by signing my copy of this letter and returning same to me. Upon receipt of your signature, I will forthwith deposit $1,000 to apply on said purchase price, together with a copy of this agreement with the escrow agent I will specify.

This offer shall be valid for 2 days.

Yours truly,
Karl Bell

I accept the foregoing offer.
Dated ....
Dalton A. Price

In this type of one–sided offer the seller is placed at a big disadvantage. The prospective buyer has placed many conditions and restrictions and given the seller no escape. You could have to wait 6 months to a year until Karl gets his loan approved. Mr. Bell has many escape clauses. If he doesn't get his loan approved, if he doesn't get the right interest rate, the payment period specified, the proper appraised value, etc. he can call off the deal. But you can't back out of the deal once you've signed.

If you must accept this type of an offer, do it with a counter–offer. Insist that the buyer be qualified for a loan, say within a week, or the deal is off. Demand that the items in paragraph 2 be completed and agreed upon within 2 to 3 days and check with a mortgage company to make sure the loan conditions specified in paragraph 1 are reasonable. Also insert a clause that escrow must close within 30 days.

When I sold my house, the interest rate kept rising. If my sale had been contingent on my buyer getting a specific interest rate, I may have had a much more difficult time closing the deal.

Let's go through these 4 offers and rank them. Since we don't know what kind of negotiations we'll be encountering, rank them in order of price:

1. Eldon Hayes........................ $55,000
2. Karl Bell $52,000
3. Joan Diffenderfer.................... $50,000
4. Horatio Alpert $40,000

The next step is to tentatively accept Mr. Hayes' offer and start negotiating the details with him. Meanwhile keep the other 3 prospects on a string for backup and tell Mr. Hayes you accept his offer and want to sign an *Agreement of Sale*, or similar form. Don't reject any offers at this point. Tell your prospects you're considering a number of offers and you'll give them your answer in a few days. Once you have officially rejected an offer, you can't go back and accept it. The rejection kills the offer.

DO I NEED A LAWYER?

If your sale is a standard, fairly simple one, you should be able to handle it without a lawyer. However, if your buyer shows up with a lawyer, you'd better hire one too.

Also, if your home sale is complex (e.g. you're subdividing your lot and only selling part of the lot with your house, or some similar complication), call a real estate lawyer in at this point to help with the negotiations. A lawyer may charge from $100 to $200 or more. Ask the lawyer to quote you a fee before you hire him or her. This fee is tax deductible from the profit you'll make on your house sale. Some states also require that a lawyer make up the *Sales Contract*. Check with your local escrow company. If you run into any complications by all means hire a lawyer.

Let's assume for now that your sale is fairly routine, as most home sales are, and that the negotiations will be between you and the buyer.

NEGOTIATION

Books have been written on the art of negotiating so don't expect to learn it all in a few paragraphs. I can only cover the highlights, but I highly recommend *How To Read a Person Like a Book* by Gerard I. Nierenberg and Henry H. Calero. This book shows how to recognize the true-attitude of a buyer by observing *Body Language*. For example, if your buyer crosses his arms over his chest, buttons his suitcoat and crosses his legs when he talks to you, he's defensive, resisting compromise, shutting you off. He's closed his mind. However, if your prospect faces you with his arms open, his coat unbuttoned, he has an open mind and is receptive to suggestion. When you're getting close to agreeing on terms, your buyer will lean toward you, trying to get closer to you.

These are but a few of the elements of *Body Language*. If you wish to pursue this subject further, I urge you to read the entire book.

In general, negotiations proceed as follows:
1. State your request.
2. Allow the buyer to comment.
3. Counter the buyer's objections with a positive statement. Ask your buyer's opinion.
4. Make a counter–offer.
5. Compromise.
6. Come to terms.

Let me illustrate this procedure by an example. Let's assume you've listed your house at $56,000. Your prospect has given you a written offer for $50,000. When you negotiate, the session should be in your house, in your best room, with the radio and TV turned off, the kids out of the way, and the telephone turned off. Keep a copy of your *Fact Sheet* handy.

To set the scene let's assume that both husbands and both wives are present, comfortablly seated at the living room table. You have the written offer in front of you.

We've considered your offer," you start out the negotiations, "but it's considerably lower than we can sell for. Our firm price is $56,000. We're already splitting the realtor's commission with you, so you're getting an extremely good price." Whenever you make a statement, back it up with some positive aspect of your particular situation.

"That may be," your buyer responds, leaning forward (this indicates he wants to get closer to you, his mind is not closed to increasing his offer). "But my wife and I have been looking at the Pizzica house down the street. Theirs is the same model as yours, and they're only asking $52,000."

"The Pizzica house is a good buy," you counter, "but for $52,000 you're not going to get as large a lot as we have." Know your competition, counter any objections with a positive statement. And remember, no 2 houses are exactly alike so they can't be compared directly. Lot sizes are different, house condition will vary, etc.

"That's true," he nods, looking at his wife for help. They both need your reassurance that they're making the right decision in buying a house. A lot of money is involved and people are understandably cautious and suspicious.

"Maybe we could go up to $54,000," the buyer's wife says hesitantly, reaching out to touch her husband's hand as he looks around the living room. She really wants this house.

"We appreciate your higher offer," your wife comes into the conversation. "And we know you'll just love the neighborhood, still $54,000 is a little low."

"But we're willing to compromise," you add to your wife's comment. "We're willing to meet you halfway."

"What do you think, honey?" the buyer asks his wife. He wants to go higher but needs her agreement.

"Can we afford $55,000?" she asks hesitantly. Again they buyers need reassurance to push them up over the edge of indecision.

"Remember the elementary school is only 2 blocks away," your wife reminds them, knowing they have 2 kids in elementary school. "And we don't have any traffic here is this cul-de-sac."

"All right," she nods, sighing. The decision is made, probably seeing her kids, lunch bucket in hand, skipping off toward the school close by.

"All right," your buyer agrees, "We'll raise our offer to $55,000."

"It's a deal," you reply, grinning. You came down only $1,000.

You shake on it, but you immediately bring out your *Agreement to Purchase*, fill it out and sign it.

SUPPOSE WE DON'T COME TO AN AGREEMENT?

You may not come to a total agreement during your first meeting. You may have to give each other some time to think over your offers and counter–offers. So be prepared for more than one meeting.

If you postpone a decision don't delay it longer than a day or so. A prospect may cool off quickly. You need to resolve a decision quickly. Remind your buyer that you'll keep your house on the market and continue to accept other offers until you both have reached a complete decision.

You may lose a buyer during negotiations but don't be discouraged. If they're especially stubborn, if their demands are unreasonable and they refuse to compromise, you should sense this and call it quits. Don't waste your energy and time with a chronic complainer who's trying to rob you of your property.

All you need is *one* buyer.

IF YOU ACCEPT AN OFFER

You've agreed on a price and you pull out your *Agreement to Purchase* similar to that shown below. It can also be called a *Binder, Purchase Agreement* or *Deposit Receipt*, or other similar title, but they're all practically the same.

Don't use any form which has the word *Contract* in its title. It's unnecessary, and that word scares people away. The form, properly executed, means *Contract* no matter what it's called.

AGREEMENT TO PURCHASE

TO: _____ *Seller's Name* _____

I, the undersigned, hereby agree to purchase from you the following described real estate in_____County, state of, to wit:

Legal description of Property _____

_____

_____

_____

at and for the price of ____ *Total price, e.g., Forty thousand dollars* ____

$40,000 _____ *upon the following terms, to wit:*

Specify your special conditions, e.g., Escrow to close in 30 days, what extras are included in purchase price, etc.

_____

_____

I hand to *Seller* _____

as earnest money on this purchase, my check for $ *500-1000*

Witness my hand this_____day of_____

19_____.

_____
PURCHASER

Signed in the Presence of:

_____WITNESS

_____WITNESS

The above agreement to purchase accepted this _____

day of _____ 19 ____. I agree to furnish an abstract

showing good and merchantable title and deliver a warranty deed to the above party.

_____

OWNER OF SAID PROPERTY

You can purchase a form similar to the above at a stationery store for a few cents.

To protect yourself, be sure specific vital information is included after the second *to wit*:

1. Escrow closing date—a 30 day escrow period is typical. Escrow has been closed in as little as a week but this takes a lot of expediting to make sure everything falls into place. Call an escrow company to get an idea of how long an average escrow takes and put that information in your agreement.

2. What fixtures, extras, etc., are included, which are excluded in the purchase price?

3. Moving out time—Generally this is at or shortly after the close of escrow, but this is a negotiable item.

4. Termite inspection—Don't volunteer to have one done. Many loan companies don't require it. If your buyers insist on one tell them they'll have to pay for it. The cost is fairly small, about $20 to $50 so it's nothing to quibble over.

5. Escrow company—Specify if you've already chosen one or state *escrow company to be chosen by mutual agreement.*

6. Proration of Costs and Expenses—This refers to how taxes, utility bills, closing costs, etc. should be pro-

rated between buyer and seller. Generally if you've lived in the house for 9 months of the year you'll be expected to pay 3/4 of the taxes for the year. Also you should pay the utility bills up until the day you move out. I believe the statement *Proration of Costs and Expenses and Closing Costs to be as determined by Escrow* to be the fairest statement to cover this aspect. Escrow companies follow standard procedures for handling these matters. They use procedures which from experience are fairest to both the buyer and seller.

7. Add any special provisions peculiar to the situation, e.g. *Loan to be obtained through Townsend Federal.*

8. For a commercial loan, if points are charged, the buyer should pay these point charges.

Once you've accepted an offer you can't back out and accept a higher one. Your house is sold so you must take it off the market. Take your *For Sale By Owner* sign down and cancel your newspaper ads. You've received $500 to $1,000 of your buyer's money as a deposit so they'll be reluctant to back out now and lose their earnest money.

Your next step should be to make a preliminary qualification of your buyer. Because this step is so intricately interwoven with home loans, I've included that information in the next chapter. If your buyer fails to qualify for a loan you must return the deposit to the buyer. If the buyer backs out you can probably keep the deposit as payment for taking your house off the market for a certain period of time.

But once you're in escrow, the chances of the deal falling through are small. By now your buyer is qualified, has a loan commitment, has invested a lot of earnest money, so you must now wait for the paper mill to grind through its inexorably slow manner.

IF YOU REJECT THE OFFER

If the offer is completely out of line, as was Mr. Alpert's, you merely write on the bottom of the offer:

I hereby reject the foregoing offer.

(signed) Anthony Jones
May 13

IF YOU MAKE A COUNTER–OFFER

If one or more of the conditions of the offer are unacceptable to you and you're not too far away from the buyer on price and other terms, you can make a counter–offer in writing. This may almost completely reduce the need for negotiations.

You may write, for example:

I hereby accept the foregoing offer with the following changes/additions:

1. The total purchase price shall be $54,250. (The buyer had offered $52,800).

2. The indicated escrow shall close within 30 days or less from the date of this offer, unless you and I both agree to extend said period.

Again you sign and date your counter–offer and give it to your prospect. If your buyer agrees and so states on the form, and if he signs and dates your counter–offer, you have an official agreement.

If your buyer doesn't agree at this point, you should forget about passing notes back and forth and sit down and verbally discuss the terms and try to negotiate and come closer in terms. If your negotiations get too complicated and involved, I urge you to call in a lawyer specializing in real estate transactions. Some people are too difficult to deal with on a one–on–one situation, so call in some legal help if you get too bogged down.

The Contract Of Sale Of Real Estate

There is no such thing as a standard real estate contract so I haven't included any sample in this book. The form, content and manner of handling these contracts vary so much from state to state it's impossible to cover it all in one book. Check with your local escrow or title company to see what form is used, how it is handled, etc. The basic law requires that agreements to buy and sell land be written and signed by the parties who are to be bound by the contract.

In some states a real estate contract can be drawn up only by a lawyer. In other states alternate documents, such as escrow instructions, the *Agreement to Purchase* illustrated earlier, or similar form can accomplish the same task.

No matter what the form, the following minimum information should be included:

1. Names of sellers and buyers. Both spouses must sign.
2. Legal description of real estate plus a listing of what personal property (drapes, carpets, etc.) are included in the sales price.
3. The purchase price, conditions, payment provisions of the loan, including the amount of deposit (earnest money).
4. Closing costs—Which costs the buyer pays, which the seller pays.
5. Possession—When the buyer will move in.
6. Prorating of closing costs for some items is generally as determined by the escrow company.

Now that your house is sold it's up to you to help your buyer get a loan. It can save a lot of time for both you and the buyer if you assist in this task.

7
HELP YOUR BUYER
GET A LOAN

Most people who buy a house must finance their purchase through a mortgage. You, the seller, should not only learn something about mortgages, but you should also assist your buyer in getting a loan.

"Why should I help my buyer get a loan?" you may ask. "I thought a loan was the buyer's responsibility."

That's true, in theory. But in practice you can save both yourself and your buyer a lot of time and money if you have some preliminary discussions with mortgage companies even before you put your house on the market.

First, your buyer probably has done little or no checking into the current loan rates, down payments, points, etc. Until your buyers have decided on a specific house, for a specific price, they may think any discussions with lenders are a waste of time.

Second, if you do preliminary checking, you'll have all the information necessary to show how much the down payment required is, how much the monthly payments will be, etc. With interest rates, down payments and points varying so much, you'll have the latest information to show the buyer. And you can also do a preliminary qualification to insure your prospect can afford your house. It can be very frustrating to feel you have your house sold, the deal all locked up and you're ready to open the champagne bottle to celebrate. Then you find out your buyer is a dreamer, full of debts and doesn't make enough money to afford your home.

"But, aren't all mortgage rates pretty much standardized, regulated by law?"

No, they're not. They vary considerably. Even though the government regulates the interest rates on FHA and VA loans, other gimmicks such as points (discussed later in this chapter) can make one loan a good one and a seemingly similar loan, with the identical interest rate, a bum deal.

Commercial loans which finance most home mortgages are only loosely regulated and can charge almost whatever the money market will bear (subject to lenient usury rates). Interest rates can easily vary from 1/4 percent to 1/2 percent from one institution to another. This may seem like a small variation, but an increased interest rate of only 1/2 percent on a 30 year, $40,000 loan means the buyer will be paying an extra $5,300 for the house merely because of this slightly higher interest rate. Also, down payments and other miscellaneous charges vary from one lending organization to another, so these should be compared.

It definitely pays for both you and the buyer to shop around for the best mortgage deal. You should call or visit at least 3 or 4 banks and the same number of savings and loan associations to get the facts and compare their competitive rates, their special charges, the time to process loans, etc. I've included as Figure 7-1 a table which lists the information you should request when you talk to loan officials at various institutions so they can be compared. Stick to reputable banks and savings and loan organizations because they're monitored by the government to protect the person who gets the loan.

WHAT ARE THE STEPS IN GETTING A LOAN?

1. The buyer makes out a loan application. A fee may be required for processing this.
2. The mortgage institution conducts a credit search and report on the buyer.
3. The lender sends out an appraiser to appraise your property.
4. The mortgage company issues a loan commitment to

the buyer insuring the buyer of getting a loan for a specific amount at a specific interest rate.

5. A Title Search is made (See Chapter 8.)
6. A note and mortgage are issued.

All of these steps are not necessarily carried out in this order and some may be carried out at the same time.

How long will it take your buyer to get a loan? Anywhere from 1 to 2 weeks or perhaps longer. It depends on the state of the money market, your buyer's credit rating, etc. Check with the loan companies to find out how much time it takes when you're in the process of selling your house.

BASICS OF LOANS

First of all don't be confused by all the terms such as first deed, deed of trust, first lien, etc. They're all legal jargon designed to confuse the general public. They all mean mortgage loan so we'll use that term.

A home mortgage loan is simply a loan given to a house buyer which uses the home as security in case the buyer defaults on the loan payments.

Since few people can afford to pay cash, most homes have long term mortgages with 20 to 30 year payment schedules. A home mortgage is one of the lowest interest rate loans available to the individual. Very few people default on home loans. Although the interest rate has climbed up and down from the 4 percent loan after World War II to as high as 11 percent, it's still the best bargain in loans.

The loan rate on cars and credit card borrowing is upwards of 18 percent because a much larger percentage of the public defaults on these loans. Also, cars often wear out before they're paid for so an auto loan provides little security for a lender.

Home mortgage loans are *amortized* which means that

the buyer pays the same monthly payment throughout the entire life of the loan. Part of this payment goes toward paying off the interest on the loan, part of the money goes toward paying off the principal (the total amount of money you still owe on the loan).

The formula for calculating monthly payments to amortize loans for various interest rates, payment periods and amounts is very complex, so I've included figure 7-2 which covers monthly payments for loans ranging from 8 percent to 13 percent and mortgage lengths from 5 to 40 years. This table shows the monthly payment required for each $1,000 of money borrowed.

For example, let's assume your buyer needs to obtain a mortgage for $50,000 and you have already checked and found out that the current going-rate for home mortgages is 10 percent on a 25 year loan. Referring to figure 7-2, the monthly payment required is $9.09 for each $1,000 borrowed. For a $50,000 loan, the monthly payment will be 50 times $9.09 or $455. Incidentally, paying this $455 a month for 25 years means the homeowner pays a total of about $136,500 for the $50,000 borrowed, that's about 273 percent of the amount of the loan. For an uneven dollar amount, for example $53,500 simply multiply 53.5 times $9.09 for a monthly payment of $486.32.

If this table is inadequate for your needs, visit a savings and loan association or a bank and tell them you're selling your house. Ask them for a copy of a little booklet entitled *Expanded Tables for Monthly Mortgage Loans* or a booklet of similar contents. They should give you one free. Or you can go to a book store and buy a copy.

These booklets list interest rates for terms ranging from 1 to 40 years and for loans ranging in size from about $100 to about $75,000 with interest rates from 6 percent to 15 percent. With these detailed tables you won't have to do any calculations. Just read the amount of the monthly payment directly out of the table.

To amortize a loan, the monthly payment is made large enough so that it not only pays off the interest, but that enough money is left over to pay on the loan amount (also called the principal). Your payments are the same every month and, at the end of the loan period, your mortgage is completely paid off.

If, for example, a buyer gets a 10 percent $40,000 loan, the simple interest in this amount is .10 times $40,000 or $4,000 per year. Divided by 12 that requires $333 per month to pay just the interest.

Now, look in Figure 7-2. To amortize a 10 percent loan for 30 years would require a payment of $8.78 per month for each $1,000 of the loan or $351 per month for the $40,000 loan. So, for the first year of the loan, $351 minus $333 or $18 per month of the payment is being applied to reducing the size of the loan.

This may seem like a small amount, but remember the loan is for 30 years and the interest is charged on the unpaid balance of the loan. Each year more and more of your monthly payment goes toward paying off the loan, less and less on interest. For example, at the end of 25 years, this $40,000 loan will be reduced to a little over $16,000.

The difference between the amount you still owe on the loan balance (the principal) and the selling price of your home is your *equity*. In the above example, if your house had increased in value to $60,000, you have an equity of $60,000 minus $16,000 in your house. You'd receive this $44,000 equity in cash when your house is sold and escrow closes.

POINTS AND MISCELLANEOUS CHARGES

Usually when you ask about obtaining a loan for a home mortgage you'll not only be quoted an interest rate, but also a certain number of *points*. Points are simply an extra fee charged by the lender, over and above the interest rate, as part of the charges of getting a loan.

LOAN COMPARISON DATA

Name of Savings &
Loan Institution or Bank _____ Address: _____

Phone: _____ Person Contacted: _____

House Selling Price: _____ Date: _____

DOWN PAYMENT		Interest Rate	Payment Period	Loan Amount	Monthly Payment	Points	Miscellaneous Charges
Percent	Amount						
†							
†							

†FHA; VA

Time to Process Loan _____ Days to Pay Off Penalty _____

Is Secondary Financing Permissible? _____

Comments: _____
_____
_____
_____

†The first 6 spaces are for the terms of conventional loans, the latter 2 for FHA and VA loans, if they're available.

Figure 7-1

MONTHLY PAYMENTS FOR EACH $1,000
OF AN AMORTIZED MORTGAGE

Percent Interest	MORTGAGE LENGTH IN YEARS							
	5	10	15	20	25	30	35	40
8	20.28	12.13	9.56	8.36	7.72	7.34	7.10	6.95
8½	20.52	12.40	9.85	8.68	8.05	7.69	7.47	7.33
9	20.76	12.67	10.14	9.00	8.39	8.05	7.84	7.71
9¼	20.88	12.80	10.29	9.16	8.56	8.23	8.03	7.91
9½	21.00	12.94	10.44	9.32	8.74	8.41	8.22	8.10
9¾	21.13	13.08	10.59	9.49	8.91	8.59	8.41	8.30
10	21.25	13.22	10.75	9.65	9.09	8.78	8.60	8.49
10¼	21.37	13.35	10.9	9.82	9.26	8.96	8.79	8.69
10½	21.49	13.49	11.05	9.98	9.44	9.15	8.98	8.89
10¾	21.62	13.63	11.21	10.15	9.82	9.33	9.18	9.08
11	21.74	13.78	11.37	10.32	9.80	9.52	9.37	9.28
11¼	21.87	13.92	11.52	10.49	9.98	9.71	9.56	9.48
11½	21.99	14.06	11.68	10.66	10.16	9.90	9.76	9.68
11¾	22.12	14.20	11.84	10.84	10.35	10.09	9.96	9.88
12	22.25	14.35	12.00	11.01	10.53	10.29	10.16	10.09
13	22.75	14.93	12.65	11.72	11.28	11.06	10.95	10.90

Figure 7-2

If you feel mathematically inclined and want to calculate it yourself, here's the complex formula:

$$P = \frac{M}{12} \left[\frac{i}{1 + (1 + i)} - n \right]$$

where P = monthly payment
  M = Mortgage loan value
  i = annual interest

BUYER QUALIFICATION

Purchase Price: _____   Interest Rate: _____

		YEARS TO REPAY LOAN			
		—	20	25	30
DOWN PAYMENT	1. Percent				
	2. Dollars				
3. Loan Total					
4. Monthly Payment					
5. Monthly Taxes and Insurance					
6. Utilities, Monthly Average					
7. Total Monthly Expenses (Add Columns 4, 5 and 6)					
8. Yearly Payment (Column 7 x 12)					
9. 4 x Column 8 (Equals Buyer's Minimum Yearly Salary)					

The first column heading is blank so you can insert any special payment
period you desire.

Figure 7-3

Sometimes it's called a *loan fee*, but call it what they
will, it's just a legal gimmick, another way of getting extra money out of the person getting the mortgage. Points
effectively increase the quoted interest rate without ap-
pearing to do so. The law permits the lender to charge as
many points as they wish to so it's unlikely points will
ever be completely eliminated in home mortgage loans.

1 point is 1 percent of the mortgage's value, i.e., $1 is
charged for every $100 borrowed. This can mount up

quite fast. 5 points on a $40,000 loan means the lender keeps .05 times $40,000 or $2,000 *just for giving the loan*. Points are a one time charge and have to be paid when the loan money is obtained. So the buyer who expects $40,000 under the above example, is only going to get a $38,000 loan.

How does this affect you, the seller?

Right in the pocketbook, that's where! If your buyer obtains a *Conventional Loan* (see page 118) you should expect and insist that your buyer pay these points. Or, you may have to compromise in your negotiations and agree to share the points equally with your buyer.

Possibly your present lender will not charge points if your buyer finances with your mortgage company. Fortunately I had this clause in my mortgage. Check with your current mortgage holder to see what their policy is.

Here's the real danger with points. If your buyer is getting an FHA or VA loan the law forbids the buyer from paying points. So the only person left to pay the points is *you, the seller*. For FHA and VA loans you'll be getting less money from your property than you've planned.

Mortgage companies also tag on all sorts of miscellaneous fees for loan applications such as credit checks, loan fees, etc. When checking with loan companies, ask them to tell you all their miscellaneous fees and list them on the table in Figure 7-1 (page 114).

WHAT IS PRIME RATE?

Before we leave the discussion of interest let me clear up the meaning of *Prime Rate* which you read so much about in the papers.

The Prime Rate is the interest rate which lenders charge their best customers, their most creditworthy clients, such as large corporations and business.

Although not directly tied into home mortgage loan rates, the prime rate is an indicator of the tightness or looseness of the money market. If the prime rate is high, it's a tight money market. Home loan interest is going to be high and loan money hard to get, although the interest rate for home mortgages may not be as high as the prime rate. Conversely, a low prime rate means that money is available and the home loan rate should be lower and more competitive.

The prime rate varies, sometimes from week to week, and over wide limits. For example, at the beginning of 1973 the prime rate was 6 percent and was increased 15 times that year. By July 1974 the prime rate reached 12 percent. In 1979 it dipped to 11½ percent.

TYPES OF LOANS

3 major types of loans are available:
1. Conventional
2. FHA
3. VA or GHI

All 3 types are made by commercial lenders, but the regulations and qualifications for each are different.

Interest rates for Conventional Loans are pretty much established by the mortgage companies. FHA loans are insured and the interest rate is regulated by the government. Interest rates are not only regulated by the government for VA loans, but the loan is also guaranteed to a certain extent.

CONVENTIONAL LOANS

Most homes are mortgaged by conventional loans. These loans, accounting for from 60 to 80 percent of all home loans, have their interest rate set by the lenders. The rate goes up and down as the money market tightens and loosens.

Downpayments may vary from 5 to 20 percent, or even higher. Loan periods of from 20 to 30 years are typical. Usually the larger the downpayment a borrower makes, the lower the interest rate. Since the borrower puts a larger downpayment into a house, the buyer is less liable to default. Typically going from a 10 percent to a 20 percent downpayment lowers the interest rate by 1/2 percent, and it lowers the points charged.

Conventional loan terms are not as generous as for FHA and VA loans since the conventional loan is usually not insured. The loan is between the lender and the home buyer. Naturally the lender stands a bigger chance of loss on such a loan.

Points are usually charged on conventional loans. These points can be paid by either buyer or seller, or shared, as discussed under *Negotiations* in Chapter 6.

Savings and loan associations usually are the best source of home mortgages and often offer about 1/4 percent lower interest rate as compared to banks. Commercial banks seem more interested in financing cars, charge accounts, personal property, etc. which return about 18 percent a year interest, about twice what a home mortgage does. And those high interest loans are paid off in shorter periods of time, typically from 1 to 3 years.

A variation of the standard conventional loan is the *Insured Conventional Loan.* These privately insured mortgages are available in some parts of the country. With this type of loan a smaller downpayment is possible. The cost for the insurance is typically 1/2 percent of the loan amount at closing and 1/4 percent payable over the next 8 years. With this loan the private insurer guarantees that the top 20 percent of the loan will be repaid. If your buyer can only make a small downpayment, say 10 percent, you should check if this type of insurance is available.

FHA LOANS

Although called FHA loans these mortgages are financed by commercial banks. The FHA does not loan money.

FHA insured loans are regulated by the Department of Housing and Urban Development through the Federal Housing Administration. Such loans made by FHA–approved lenders permit the purchase of a home with a very low downpayment. Houses are financed, based on their FHA appraised value.

The resulting mortgages are insured by the FHA by collecting 1/2 percent on the unpaid balance for the life of the loan. This 1/2 percent insurance fee is in addition to the interest rate charged by the lender. Anyone is eligible for an FHA loan. They were initially started to aid low income families to buy homes with low downpayments. Since the FHA mortgage insurance protects the lender against loss, slightly more liberal mortgage terms are available. FHA insured loans provide for lower downpayments (as low as 3 percent on homes costing $25,000) and lower interest rates (often about 1/2 percent lower than conventional loans). Loans can be made for periods as long as 35 years, up to 15 percent of the loan can be prepaid in 1 year without a penalty.

This sounds great for the buyer but there are some big disadvantages for the seller of the home. First, to make up for the lower interest rates the lender charges points which the seller must pay. A second disadvantage is that typical government paperwork and delays are involved and it may take up to 2 months to process and obtain an FHA appraisal, paperwork, inspections, etc. Another potential problem is that the FHA appraiser will inspect your house and perhaps list certain repairs and inspection services which *must* be done before the FHA will permit the loan to be given.

If possible, avoid FHA loans because of the point penalty and the time delays. However, sometimes a seller is not in a position to select buyers so you may have to accomodate an FHA buyer. If you do, insist on a quick response by stating in your sales contract that unless the loan is approved in say 2 weeks the sales contract is void. Imposing a deadline usually makes people work a little harder to process the paperwork. Also, get an FHA appraisal just as soon as your house is ready to be put on the market. Waiting periods for FHA appraisals can be from 2 weeks to 2 months.

Also, in your negotiations with a buyer, you can't afford to come down as much in price with an FHA Loan as you could with a conventional loan because you'll be paying the point penalty. And you can't charge more for the house than the FHA appraisal. So, bargain shrewdly and toughly if your customer insists on an FHA-insured loan. If you must sell at the appraised value you may be getting much less for your home than you've expected.

There is little to be served in listing the current interest rate, points, maximum loan guarantee, etc. since these factors change so often. But, be prepared and check with loan agencies or write or call the nearest FHA office and they'll send you free pamphlets, to find out the latest information on FHA loans.

VA OR GHI LOANS

VA loans are also obtained through commercial lending institutions. However, the Veterans' Administration guarantees payment of a substantial part of the loan in case of default.

These loans are available to eligible veterans. But, once issued, they can be taken over by a non-veteran.

Again, because of the security of these loans being guaranteed by the government, interest rates are lower than conventional loans, payoff times are longer and, if the lender is agreeable, for some loans no downpayment is required. Because the government guarantees the mortgage, VA approved loans do not charge the extra 1/2 percent insurance the FHA does, so the VA loan rate is lower by this 1/2 percent. Usually the VA and FHA loan rates are the same, except for the added 1/2 percent on the FHA insurance. Commercial lenders also charge points for VA loans. These have been as high as 12 percent. By law the seller must pay the point penalty, and it may take as long as 2 months to process VA loan applications.

Much of the same advice given under FHA loans above also applies to VA loans. A VA appraisal is required and should be requested as soon as possible. The cost is under $65. The VA may also require that certain repairs be accomplished before a loan can be granted.

If you have already have a VA loan, a non-veteran can assume your loan. A VA loan may be paid off in full, or by partial lump sums without penalty. Typically the VA guarantees that up to $25,000 of an approved loan (or 60 percent if that is less) will be repaid. There is no limit to the amount of a loan the VA will approve. But the maximum guarantee, in case of default, is $25,000.

Since the rates and regulations governing VA guaranteed loans also change so frequently, if you're considering permitting a VA loan, use the same precautions discussed under FHA loans. Contact the local or regional VA office for information and contact a lender for their specific VA guaranteed loan regulations and rates.

TRAPS TO WATCH FOR

Although the loan is legally your buyer's responsibility, you can help your buyer avoid some traps which occasionally appear in loan documents. Some also affect the seller.

Many loan companies include a payoff penalty in their loans. This means that if the person who borrowed the money originally tries to pay the loan off early, the borrower will have to pay a penalty. On my home loan this amounted to 6 months interest. Some loans require a prepayment penalty of 3 percent of the unpaid balance. This is usually a few hundred dollars which the seller has to pay to clear out the loan, so this comes out of *your* pocket.

Some loan companies do not charge a payoff penalty or points if the buyer obtains a new mortgage at the same institution at which you have your old mortgage so this is worth looking into. You could save money if your buyer finances with your mortgage company. Check with your lender to find out their policy. Usually there is no payoff penalty for a second mortgage, but check with your loan company to verify this if you have such a mortgage.

Some loans have *escalator* clauses. This escalator clause permits the mortgage company to change the interest rate, up or down, without the borrowers' consent, as business conditions change. This is a very dangerous and unfair clause and should be avoided at all costs.

QUALIFY YOUR BUYER

Although the mortgage company will do the official qualification of the buyer, it helps the seller to make a quick check on the financial qualifications of your prospective buyer. This way you won't have to waste time with the dreamers who can't afford your home. You can concentrate on those who can.

There are many rules of thumb which loan agents use to qualify buyers. People differ so much in the way they spend their money, pay their debts, etc. that these are only rough guidelines.

Still these guidelines should help eliminate most of

the dreamers who have no business wasting your time and crushing your hopes by bidding on your house and then finding out they can't qualify. In my own experience, about half of the people who appeared sincere in bidding our house could not qualify financially. I was amazed at the lack of knowledge of interest rates, downpayment requirements, monthly payments etc. involved in buying a home.

In the first week of selling our house, a sincere couple made a bid on our house and we accepted verbally. We were happy, ready to celebrate, but my second sense told me to send the buyer down to the lender, right away. We found out the next day the buyer couldn't qualify and were very discouraged. You can save yourself some disappointment if you do this preliminary qualification.

One old rule of thumb is that a person can afford a house which costs 3 times that person's yearly salary. Thus, someone making $20,000 a year could, by this guideline, afford a $60,000 house.

Another guideline is that the monthly payment on a house (this includes the monthly mortgage payment plus monthly taxes plus monthly house insurance plus average monthly utilities) should be less than 1 week's take home pay. Consider this example of a prospect who requires a $24,000 mortgage. The current interest rate is 10 percent and a 30 year loan is available. From the interest tables the monthly mortgage payment is $211, the yearly taxes on the house are $480, the monthly utilities average $50 and the yearly insurance premium is $240.

Monthly mortgage payment $211
Monthly taxes ($480 divided by 12)........... 40
Monthly utilities average.................... 50
Monthly insurance ($240 divided by 12)....... 20
                                   TOTAL $321

Thus, if your buyer's weekly take-home pay is over $321, that prospect should be able to afford a $24,000 mortgage.

Incidentally, an FHA study showed that average homeowners spend 26 percent of their monthly income on mortgage payments, insurance, utilities, repairs and taxes. 23 percent is about a week's salary, so this guideline is a conservative one.

To apply this rule of thumb to your specific situation, consider figure 7-3. Fill in the purchase price where indicated, the interest rate, the downpayment in percent and dollars on lines 1 and 2 and the remaining loan balance on line 3.

From figure 7-2 find the amount a buyer must pay per month for each $1,000 of the loan. Mulitply this monthly payment figure times the thousands of dollars from line 3. Enter this monthly payment on line 4.

From you *Fact Sheet* fill in the taxes, insurance and utilities as indicated on lines 5 and 6. Add lines 4, 5, and 6 to get line 7, the total monthly payments the person who buys your home will incur.

If you multiply this monthly payment by 12, you'll get the yearly housing cost for line 8. Finally multiply this yearly payment by 4 to find out the minimum yearly take-home salary your prospect must earn to be able to afford your house.

You may want to repeat this procedure for a few different interest rates, downpayments and loan repayment periods. Then you should be prepared to discuss this with your buyer. If your prospect refuses to reveal his or her yearly salary, simply show them the sheet and they'll get the message.

Remember, this is only a rough guideline. The final judgment, the final qualification must be made by a loan company. If your prospect is close to this qualification figure, encourage your buyer to hurry on down to the mortgage company and have them further examine the prospect's qualifications. Although a full credit check will take 3 to 4 days, a skilled loan application officer can tentatively qualify a prospect in less than an hour's time.

When I sold my house, after getting discouraged over the first prospect's inability to qualify, I refused to even seriously consider offers until the prospect had been tentatively qualified by a lender. Although buying a house is a person's largest lifetime investment, people know woefully little about such matters.

This qualification technique can also be worked in reverse. If you start with the prospect's yearly salary on line 9 and divide by 4, you have line 8. Divide line 8 by 12 and you have line 7, the total monthly expenses your prospect can afford. You already have lines 5 and 6 from your *Fact Sheet*, so subtracting lines 5 and 6 from line 7 gives you line 4, the monthly payment your prospect can afford.

Next you'll have to do some trial and error calculations, assume different repayment periods for your available interest rate. Finally you'll end up with the maximum loan a person can make and buy your house, based on the buyer's specific salary. This then gives you the downpayment the prospect has to make to buy your home.

SHOULD YOU GIVE A SECOND MORTGAGE?

If your buyer can't raise the necessary downpayment and you have no other good prospects, you may have to consider giving the buyer a second mortgage. A second mortgage is simply another mortgage, over and above the first mortgage a buyer obtains from the lending institution. First, though, you should be aware of some points about second mortgages.

Some lenders will not permit a buyer to obtain a second mortgage, so check with the mortgage company before you entertain thoughts about second mortgages.

Next, a second mortgage is exactly what the name implies. If the loan must be foreclosed because of default of the loan, the first mortgage holder has first call on the money realized from resale of the house, the holder of the second mortgage gets what's left over, if anything. VA and FHA supervised loans do not permit second mortgages.

Many second mortgages are non-amortized, that is the borrower simply pays the interest for a period of years (typically 5 years). Then, at the end of this period, the borrower has to pay off the entire second mortgage amount in case. This is called a *balloon payment*.

I've only briefly covered some of the aspects of second mortgages here. If you're seriously entertaining giving a buyer a second mortgage (and it might be a good investment for your extra capital), check into this subject more thoroughly in other reference books. Perhaps you should contact a lawyer, too.

You may be able to sell your second mortgage some time later to a mortgage company, or someone who has money to invest, but you'll probably have to sell it at a discount, so you won't get all your money back on the second mortgage.

WHAT ABOUT THE EXISTING MORTGAGE

If your equity is low and if the interest rate on your current mortgage is lower than the prevailing rate, you may find a customer who wants to take over your loan.

Some loan companies won't permit this, however, so check with your lender. If they permit it, without too large a payoff penalty, it may well be worth it to your buyer.

To take over a loan, a buyer must make a downpayment equal to the equity you have in your house. If your equity is but a few thousand dollars, this may attract a buyer.

But, if you consider this method of helping a buyer finance, make sure when your buyer takes over your loan, the buyer signs a release and takes over full responsibility for the loan. If the buyer refuses to sign such a release and later defaults on the loan, you are legally liable. See a lawyer and get help in drawing up such an agreement if you want to go this financing route.

If you have an FHA loan, a qualified buyer may take it over, but it may cost you about 1 percent of the loan balance as a fee for the paperwork involved. VA loans are also transferable, but the VA must approve the buyer. A release should also be obtained for FHA and VA loans so you're no longer responsible if the buyer defaults.

Now that your buyer is all set, let's see what escrow can do for you.

8
LEARN ABOUT ESCROW

This chapter is not intended to be a complete discussion of the many functions escrow serves. An entire book could be written on that subject alone. Here I'll give you a quick look at most of the tasks escrow accomplishes, as it applies to you. Since escrow functions and regulations vary from state to state, you should visit your local escrow company. Discuss with them ahead of time what their charges will be, what documents they need, what charges are negotiable between buyer and seller, etc.

WHAT IS ESCROW?

An escrow company is a neutral third party brought into your real estate transaction to insure that both the buyer and seller live up to their agreements. And, more importantly, escrow takes care of having all the miscellaneous documents signed and recorded, payments prorated, and accounts for all the money involved. Escrow holds the *stakes* until the buyer and seller have all the necessary conditions and all the necessary paperwork has been taken care of.

"Do I really need escrow?" you may ask. "Couldn't I take of all the tasks they accomplish and save myself the escrow fees?"

You could in theory complete the sale of your house without escrow. But it would be a dangerous undertaking and would require a lot of knowledge of the legal aspects of real estate. It would take a lot of your time. And, most dangerous of all, you could mishandle the transaction, make mistakes and end up losing a lot of money. FHA and VA loans *must* be handled by escrow.

Although my total closing costs for my house were around $700, only $150 of that was the escrow fee for handling all the paperwork. It was one of the best bargains I've ever had in my life. I highly recommend using escrow. Actually I consider escrow a necessity.

An escrow department may be part of a title company, a bank, or a savings and loan association. Privately owned and operated escrow offices are also available. If possible, use the escrow office which is associated with the savings and loan association where the buyer obtains the mortgage, or pick a title or escrow company recommended by the loan company. They're used to working together and things will go much smoother.

How long will escrow take? It's possible to speed escrow up to a week. But it takes almost a full–time job of expediting to make sure everything falls in place. It's better to allow a month for escrow, and you should call or visit your escrow agent at least once a week to insure that everything is progressing according to schedule.

What Does Escrow Do?

Once you and the buyer have agreed on the terms of the sale and on the method of financing, escrow goes to work.

Take your sales contract (sales agreement or whatever document you and your buyer have negotiated) into escrow. The escrow agent will collect the deposit from the buyer and, with buyer and seller present, will prepare a document appropriately entitled *Escrow Instructions* which states the requirements and conditions of the sale, e.g. purchase price, deposit, legal description of property, what conditions buyer and seller are to meet, etc. Both husbands and wives (if they're co-owners) must sign this agreement.

Escrow then orders a policy of title insurance to protect the buyer and the lender. Title insurance is a fee paid to a title company, which in turn conducts a title search of the real estate records in the county courthouse. The title company makes sure that you, the seller, has a clear title to the property you're selling. Claims against your property could include an easement (the right of way across your land, such as utility companies have), an unpaid mortgage, a lien against your property (e.g. a mechanic's lien for a contractor's bill you haven't paid), delinquent taxes, etc.

The escrow company will also prepare a grant deed for you to sign. They'll see that the buyer signs the necessary mortgage papers and the promissory note for repayment of the loan.

Escrow receives the money from the lender, collects the remainder of the down payment from the buyer, allocates the points as instructed (or as regulated by law), etc. In addition escrow services include handling and paying the money for inspection services, title insurance, and any special debts owed on the property. They make sure that all of these debts are accounted for before closing the deal.

After all the necessary documents and policies are filed and the money paid into the escrow account, escrow then records the necessary documents, prorates the costs for taxes, insurance, etc. When all the necessary conditions are met, escrow pays out all the money for inspection services, title insurance, points, recording fees, etc. Finally you'll be given a check for the equity you have in your house, less the fees and liens you owed on your property.

With all the above tasks to accomplish, it's easy to see why escrow is essential and why it takes about 30 days to accomplish. And, because some tasks may take longer than expected and may run into some snags, it's difficult to set and guarantee a specific date for closing escrow.

Since you don't know an exact closing date, it's difficult to plan to move out of your house. You need some time to get ready for this big move. Also you won't receive any of the money for your house until closing time. Therefore, you should insist in your sales contract that you be permitted to occupy the house until say 10 days after closing, and rent free.

You'll need these 10 days to arrange for turning off your utilities, to finish packing if you're going to move yourself, or for arranging for a moving company to move you. And you need time to straighten out your financial affairs, perhaps you're moving into another house and need part or all of the money for a down payment. Plus, there are a host of little details which crop up which you must also take care of.

For these reasons, specify in your negotiations that you'll move out 10 days or so after close of escrow. Even though your buyer officially owns your house after closing time, try to talk them into letting you stay, rent free. If that fails, you may have to compromise and pay rent for those few days. No matter what, don't try to move out on closing day, it's just too difficult to plan and execute.

CLOSING COSTS

Closing costs include all the expenses involved in the purchase of a house as described above. They may vary anywhere from $500 to $1,500 and upward. Usually the buyer pays the biggest burden of closing costs, unless the seller is stuck with paying a high burden of points. There may be as many as 20 items included in the closing costs, some must be paid by the seller, some by the buyer, some are negotiable.

Because of the wide variation of laws from state to state, it's impossible to list all the closing costs which could be charged, so I'll list only the more common ones. Visit your escrow company and they'll give you a fairly accurate estimate of what your share of the closing costs will be and they'll also be able to tell you which closing costs are negotiable in your particular state.

PRORATED COSTS

Certain costs of owning a house, such as taxes, special assessments, insurance, etc. are often paid either after or ahead of time, or in lump sums. To be fair to both you and the buyer, these costs should be prorated, using the close of escrow as the basis.

For example, if you're moving out of your house on September 1, you should pay 8/12 of that year's taxes, insurance and special assessments since you lived in the house for 8/12 of a year. The buyer should pay the other 4/12 to cover the 4 months the buyer will occupy the house. The escrow company calculates this prorating and will include these figures in the final settlement costs.

TYPICAL SELLER'S COSTS

Listed below are the typical costs which you, the seller, are expected to pay. Again this may vary from state to state, so check your escrow company to make sure.

1. Your attorney's fees.
2. Points if your buyer has an FHA or VA loan.
3. Prepayment penalty if your mortgage has such a clause in it.
4. *Title Search and Insurance Policy*—this insures you have a clear title to your property to hand over to the buyer. In some states the seller must pay this fee. Costs of this policy vary from $3.50 to $5.00 per $1,000 of sale price, that's $140 to $200 on a $40,000 house.
5. *Escrow Fees*—this is the direct fee the escrow company charges you for handling all the paperwork, finances, and taking care of all the multitude of details. This is probably your best investment in the entire transaction.

6. *Revenue Stamps* (state tax stamps)—some states use this tax assessed at the rate of $1.10 per $1,000 of house sale price. That's $44 on a $40,000 house.

7. Miscellaneous repairs specified by the buyer, VA or FHA in your purchase agreement or sales contract.

8. Mortgage payment to date of closing.

9. All liens, unpaid taxes, etc. existing against your property.

There will be other miscellaneous fees such as recording fee, reconveyance fee, statement fee, each of which cost from $5 to $20.

For closing, all of the seller's charges are added up, subtracted from your equity, and you're given a check for the balance.

TYPICAL BUYER'S COSTS

Listed below are the typical buyer's closing costs. Some of these may not be included in your particular state. Some may have to be paid by the seller.

In closing, the escrow company collects the following money from the buyer:

1. Remainder of the downpayment. That is, the total downpayment less the deposit or earnest money the buyer has already applied.

2. Credit report to establish buyer's credit rating. This costs about $10.

3. Lawyers' fees for buyer and lender.

4. Appraisal fee—typically $50 to $100.

5. *Title Search and Insurance Policy*—see under *Seller's Costs* above.

6. Termite inspection. If buyer requests it buyer should pay for it. Some loan companies do not require this. VA and FHA require a termite inspection if the house is more than 5 years old. The cost will run anywhere from $30 to $75.

7. Survey of the property is often not necessary. Cost could run from $25 to $50.

8. State mortgage tax. Some states charge this tax, it's usually about 1/2 percent $5 per $1000.
9. The mortgage recording fee for public records costs about $10.
10. The deed recording fee for courthouse records costs about $10.
11. Escrow fees are often split between buyer and seller.
12. The mortgage processing fee (service fee, loan fee, or whatever the lender cals it). This is the price the lender charges for giving the buyer a loan.
13. Prorated taxes, any special assessments.
14. The fire insurance is prorated or the new owner procures a new policy.

The buyer has to pay all these costs before closing can be accomplished.

NEGOTIABLE FEES

Listed below are some of the closing costs which can be negotiated between the buyer and the seller. Again this may vary from state to state, so check locally:
1. Points on conventional loans.
2. Rent, if the seller lives in the house after closing.

THE CLOSING

At the closing time, that magic moment, the buyer and seller sign and exchange documents and the title passes to the buyer.

You no longer own the house. Deposit the check, draw out enough money for a good celebration and take the family out for champagne, steak and lobster. You've all earned it.

9
WHAT TO DO
WHILE YOU WAIT
FOR ESCROW TO CLOSE

Even though your escrow may not close for a whole month, you still have a lot of work to do. Make a list, plan the tasks and see that everything gets done in plenty of time. Don't leave a lot of things for the last few days, or you'll never get them done properly and your move will be a frantic, painful experience.

WHAT HAS TO BE DONE BEFORE MOVING?

I'll list below some of the things which will keep you busy during the last month or so that you live in your house. This is not intended to be all inclusive, but a suggested list of the most common items to take care of. By all means make a list and schedule the tasks you have to get done. You'll be amazed at all the little details which pop up and have to be taken care of that you forgot about.

1. Call all utility companies.
2. Get ready for visit by the appraiser.
3. Get ready for the termite inspector and any other inspectors who'll be visiting your house.
4. Complete any necessary repairs.
5. Hold a *Garage Sale*.
6. Make an information list for your buyer.
7. If you're moving and packing yourself, get busy and read Chapter 10.

CALL UTILITIES AND DELIVERY PEOPLE

Call the electric, gas, phone and any other companies which service you and find out how much notice they'll need to turn off your utilities. You may not know at this time the exact date you're going to move, but you'll know approximately when. As soon as you know your exact date, call them and give them the date so you won't have your gas, electricity and phone turned off until the day *after* you move. They'll want to know where to mail your closing bills, so give them your forwarding address, if you have one.

If you're moving to another town and don't have a forwarding address, you can use General Delivery at the new address until you get established.

Close your local charge accounts, your savings and checking accounts if you're leaving town.

Make a list of all the places you have to call to give your forwarding address and check them off so you won't forget which you called and which you didn't.

Go to the post office and fill out a change of address form. If you're moving to another city or to a different address within the same city, you can specify which mail you want forwarded and which you don't. All first class mail will be forwarded to you, free of charge, for a period of one year. Second class (magazines and newspapers), if you request them, will be forwarded at additional cost for a period of 90 days. That gives you 3 months at your new address to fill in change of address cards and send them into the magazines and newspapers.

Any third class mail (also called bulk mail or junk mail) which is of obvious value can also be forwarded if you request it. However you'll have to pay additional postage. Charges are a function of weight.

All parcels, fourth class, of obvious value are forwarded, with postage due to be paid by you, unless you or the sender direct otherwise. The extra charge depends on the weight and the distance to be forwarded.

If you refuse to pay the postage due on second, third or fourth class mail, the postmaster at the forwarding address will discontinue forwarding any more of that class mail. So you can't be selective of what you want forwarded of a particular class of mail. You must accept all or none.

When I moved I refused to have the third class mail forwarded and I got lost from a lot of undesirable mailing lists I'd been wanting to get off for years, but never quite knew how. Of course moving is a rather drastic way to get off someone's list.

BEFORE THE APPRAISER COMES

Soon after your buyer has made a loan application (often within a few days), an appraiser from the loan company (or a freelance appraiser hired by them) will come out to see if your house is worth what you sold it for.

Although appraisers claim their estimates are not affected by an untidy, dirty house I don't believe them. To a certain extent appraisal is a matter of opinion. If the house looks clean and neat to the appraiser you have some pluses working for you.

Try to find out from the loan company a little ahead of time when the appraiser will be coming, then put your house back into the shape it was when the buyer saw your house. The appraiser will inspect your yard, your fences, measure the outside of your house to check the square footage and will tour the house, looking at the attic, the basement, each room to get a general idea of the condition of your house. Then, before leaving, the appraiser will ask you what you sold the house for. If everything comes out all right, the appraiser's figure will magically come out to be the exact price you sold it for.

Since appraisers can't estimate any closer than 5 or 10 percent the value of your house, they'll likely give you the benefit of the doubt and appraise your house at what you sold it for. Unless your house is way out of line in price, you're all set.

BEFORE THE TERMITE INSPECTOR COMES

If the buyer has insisted on a termite inspection you pretty much have to go along with it. The buyer should pay the bill for the inspection but you should insist on getting a little notice before the inspector comes.

Your house may have termites and you may not have even noticed it. In a survey made in New York City in an area of houses 10 years and older, termites infested nearly 60 percent of these houses. Nearly all states in the United States have termite infestation. So many loan institutions insist on this inspection.

You obviously are not qualified to make a preliminary termite inspection. But there are some things you *can* do before the inspector comes which will save you money. Since I suffer from claustrophobia, I had my two teenaged sons crawl under our house (we had no basement). They took out all the boards, bricks, the accumulation of lint from the dryer vent, and everything foreign from under the house. Much of it had been there since the house had been built.

If you don't do this the termite inspector, even though he finds no evidence of termites, will probably stick you with a *general cleanup* for which they'll charge you, the seller, from $50 to $100.

The termite inspector will check the soil condition, the foundation, porches, steps, ventilation, the shower stall (to make sure it drains properly and doesn't cause wood rot), the attic, the basement, and even the garage. They make a pretty thorough inspection which may take an hour or two.

If the inspector finds something amiss, if termite infestation if found, you'll have to see that work is done and the situation remedied. The inspector will make a return trip to insure that everything is fixed. If you have work to do and must hire someone to do it, get at least 2 independent bids for comparison.

Finally, after everything passes inspection, you'll get a copy of the report in the mail with the nice words *No evidence of active infestation, infection or adverse conditions were found.*

COMPLETE ANY NECESSARY REPAIRS

You may have some necessary repairs to make before your buyer moves in. For example, one clause in your sales contract may have said "All appliances shall be in working order." If any don't work you'll have to fix them or hire someone to fix them. It's best to arrange these repairs yourself. If your buyer moves in and the appliances don't work, the buyer will hire someone to fix them, unconcerned about the cost. And you will have to pay the bill.

Also you may need to make some repairs which the FHA or VA appraiser has stated in the appraisal report (e.g. loose shingles, broken window, etc.). Take care of these also. Again, if you hire help, get 2 bids on the cost.

HOLD A GARAGE SALE

You're going to be moving soon so take another critical look and decide which furniture, clothes, appliances, knickknacks, dishes, etc., you can do without.

Whether you move yourself, or hire someone to move you, you can save money 2 ways by holding a garage sale. You'll not only save the cost and time of packing it, you can sell it and pocket the money.

Get a pad and pencil and go through your house carefully and make a list of all the items you'd like to sell. Perhaps you have some clothes your kids have outgrown, a tricycle your teenager can't fit on anymore, a second toaster you've stored in the attic. List everything on your pad, then both busband and wife should sit down and agree that each item on the list should be sold.

Next clear a place in your garage and haul all of your

saleables out to the garage. Take a good look at everything, clean everything which needs it and set prices on the items. If you have trouble deciding what some of the items are worth, pay a quick visit to a thrift store. Since you want to move your things quickly (plan on a two-day garage sale), price your items below the going rate. Write the price on masking tape and affix the tape to each item.

Be sure you put the sizes on shoes and clothing. You may want to bundle some things together, a set of cooking pans for example, and sell them as a unit.

If you have house plants, seriously consider selling them. A mover can't transport house plants, and if you're moving yourself from one state to another, you may not be able to transport these plants beyond the stateline.

You may want to combine your saleable items with one or more neighbors and hold a gigantic garage sale. That way you'll attract a lot more customers.

Schedule your garage sale for a weekend, preferably on a Saturday and a Sunday. Put an ad in your local paper ahead of time and list a few of the outstanding items you have for sale (e.g. refrigerator, mini-bike, etc.) in your ad to draw the customers in. Reread chapter 4 on how to write a good ad.

Arrange your items neatly, group the clothing together (put the clothing on hangers or fold neatly), the books together, make aisles for your customers to walk through as they browse. Be sure you put some *Not For Sale* tags on some of the things in your garage you're not including in your sale.

On the first day of your sale, put out some signs, one on the nearest thoroughfare if you can, stating *Garage Sale* and include your address on the sign. Put a few other signs with the same information around the neighborhood and hang a large banner or sign over your garage door announcing *Garage Sale*.

Have plenty of change handy for the garage sale. You

don't want to lose sales because you can't break a $10 or $20 bill. Note the sale price in your notebook and check off each item when it's sold. You may have to do some dickering on prices, but that's just a part of doing business.

Your policy should be that everything is sold in an as is condition and that you will not permit any returns or exchanges. *Let the Buyer Beware* is the axiom of garage sales.

On the second day of your sale reduce all the prices. If your items didn't sell during the first day, maybe they were over-priced. Cross out the old price on the masking tape (so the customer can still read the old price) and write in the new lower price. Then your buyers will be getting a double bargain.

If you have the time to continue beyond a second day, go ahead, but two days should just about do it. Besides, you have other things to do.

After your sale is over, donate your left over usable discards to your favorite charity. Get a receipt to be used for income tax purposes.

Finally, take all the items not even the charity could take (old sofas for example) and haul them to the city dump. There's no need to even clutter-up your place any longer with extra junk because you'll be moving soon. The less you have to pack and carry, the better your move will be.

PERTINENT DATA FOR YOUR BUYER

Very likely your buyer will not be familiar with your neighborhood, so it would be a fine gesture to make up a list of pertinent data for your new buyer to use.

Give the buyer the name of the contact for the local Welcome Wagon. They're an excellent organization which truly welcomes people to a new community. They've welcomed us to 3 new cities and we love them.

Make a list of all the utilities which serve you, the phone numbers, etc. On the list include the paper boy's (or girl's) and the babysitter's names and numbers. Perhaps you can include the name of your family doctor. List the days the trash is picked up and the names of any servicemen you've dealt with and been satisfied with, e.g. plumber, TV repairman, etc. Leave brief instructions for operating all of the applicances and leave the instruction books, maintenance manuals, warranties and guarantees for all of the built-in appliances. You might also leave any special instructions for your lawn shrubbery, trees, grass, etc. Finally list your neighbors names to help your buyer get acquainted in the new neighborhood.

IF YOU STAY IN AFTER ESCROW CLOSES

Even though you're still living in the house after escrow closes, the house no longer belongs to you. You are a guest, a renter, so act accordingly.

You can't make any changes to the property (e.g. put up shelves, take down shelves, pull out shrubs, etc.) since the house now belongs to someone else and your new owners expect everything to stay in the same condition it was when they bought the house.

If any appliances break down, if any damage is done to the house when you're still living in it, you must see that it's repaired and pay for it.

SHOULD YOU LET YOUR BUYER
MOVE IN BEFORE ESCROW CLOSES?

If at all possible *do not* let your buyer move in before escrow closes. At this point your buyer can still back out of the deal. After living in the house, the buyer may suddenly find all kinds of things wrong with the house, the master bedroom isn't big enough, the faucet drips in the sink, etc. The buyer may even damage one of your appliances and claim it never worked. At this point a buyer can be generally obstreperous. This will be the buyer's last chance to find fault and try to get things corrected which they didn't see before, things which weren't in the sales contract.

For FHA and VA loans buyers can concoct excuses to disqualify themselves from the loan and then demand and get their money back. Then you have a house to sell all over again.

If you can possibly avoid it, don't let your buyer move in until after escrow closes.

Still, there are times when you can't avoid it. Your buyers may insist in the negotiations that they move in or they won't buy your house. It may be the only offer you have, so you'll have to agree to let them move in before closing.

However, if they do move in prior to escrow closing, insist on executing a pre-occupancy agreement. Get together with a lawyer and make one up and take the following precautions as a minimum:

1. Make sure your buyer is financially qualified to buy your house. You don't want them living in your house for a month or 2, then suddenly find out they can't qualify. You'd have to make them move out, clean up their mess and sell your house all over again. Only this time you'd have to sell a house without any furniture in it which is much harder. And you've lost a lot of time.

2. Make sure your buyer gives a substantial deposit, about 10 percent of the cost of the house, to insure that no damage is done to your house. Also, the deposit should be forfeited and given to you in case the buyer backs out of the deal.

3. Your buyer should not be permitted to make any changes or modifications to your house until after closing. It's still your house until escrow closes.

4. The buyer must pay you rent. Rent per month is

typically 1/2 to 1 percent of the sales price of the house. That's $350 to $700 per month on a $70,000 house.

5. The house is accepted in an as is condition. The buyers can't suddenly discover all sorts of new things which are wrong in their estimation and demand that you fix them or they'll back out of the deal.

6. Utility bills are to be prorated on the basis of the day the buyer moves in.

Now that you've taken care of all this and the day of escrow closing is approaching, you have to move out soon. Should you move yourself? Hire someone to move you? Pack your own things? Chapter 10 will answer these questions plus some of the tax considerations of your house sale.

10
GET READY, GET SET, MOVE

If you plan on moving only a short distance, you can rent a truck and move yourself a little at a time in many trips. Or you can hire a commercial mover and get it all over with in a few hours. When moving a considerable distance (a few hundred miles or more) you can probably only afford to make one trip and the moving problem is more complex.

I'll cover the basic aspects of both types of moves in this chapter. Much of what I've included applies to both long and short distance moves, although you needn't do much packing for short moves, especially those under about 25 miles.

Moving yourself can be a big job, but you'll save a lot of money doing it. When I moved my family from California to Oklahoma, we did all of our own packing, loading and rented a move-it-yourself truck. We drove 1500 miles and then unpacked at our destination. The total cost for the truck rental, moving equipment, gas, etc. was about $600. Before deciding to move myself, I got a bid from a reputable moving company. They would have packed and moved me for an estimated $2,000.

It was a lot of work, but we saved $1,400 moving ourselves. I, who usually drive a VW bettle, had to drive a loaded, 24 foot, cab—over—engine truck for 1500 miles. And I'd never driven a truck before. We made the trip without any mishaps in a time of a little over 3 days. We ended up with only a small scratch on our old refrigerator and a scratch on a wooden chair.

IF YOUR MOVE IS A LOCAL ONE

If it is a matter of 50 miles or less, moving considerations are much different.

First of all, state–to–state moves are regulated by the Interstate Commerce Commission and so are the moving rates. Most moving companies on such a move will charge about the same. But a local mover, if you hire a mover, has a few laws regulating him. Pick one with great care.

Long distance moves are based on the weight of your household goods, plus the mileage. Local movers usually charge an hourly rate for 2 or 3 men, plus an extra charge for mileage. If possible, use a nationally known mover who also does short distance hauls. Be sure you get insurance for your move. Beware of the mover who'll quote you a ridiculously low price. Then the hidden costs will add up to more than those quoted to you by a reasonable and well-known mover.

A rule of thumb to estimate the cost of a local move is that you will be charged about $75 per room, plus about $75 in mileage for a 25 mile move. For a 7 room house, this local move would cost about $600. These costs do not include any packing or insurance, or handling any special items such as a piano.

If you chose to move yourself, you have many alternatives. You can rent a truck, a dolly and furniture pads and move everything yourself, in 1 or more trips. Or you can rent a trailer to haul the major items in a few trips and make a lot of trips carrying smaller items in your car.

You may wish to hire some professionals to move only your heavy furniture and appliances, then move everything else yourself.

How you move depends on your budget, your back muscles, and the time you have available to move. Explore all of the above possibilities and choose the ones which best suit your pocketbook, your time and efforts. One person can't do such a move alone. You need at least one other person with muscle.

For A Long Distance Move

For a long distance move, investigate the relative costs and convenience of moving yourself or hiring a moving company.

To get started, call 2 or 3 nationally known movers and ask them to come to your house to give you a moving estimate. They'll do this free and will probably give you some booklets which will help you plan your move. And they'll give you a copy of *Summary of Information for Shippers of Household Goods* which is published by the Interstate Commerce Commission. A professional moving company representative will go through your house, noting everything you wish to move, and come up with a total number of cubic feet of items involved in the move.

I had a 7 room house and the agent estimated 1080 cubic feet of items to be moved. Then, by estimating that my items would average about 7 pounds per cubic foot, the total cargo would be about 7,500 pounds, which he rounded off to 8,000 pounds. The rate from California to Oklahoma at that time was $19.06 per 100 pounds, so the basic charge was $1,525 for the move alone. But insurance was extra, amounting to $50 (based on 50 cents per $100 valuation, a total valuation of $10,000 for all my worldly possessions).

But that wasn't all. The charge for packing and the boxes used was nearly $450. And, by law, a mover is permitted to be within 10 percent of that estimate. So my total tab was estimated to be over $2,000. I would have had to pay in cash or with a certified check before my furniture would be unloaded at my destination.

There's still a hooker to this. What the mover gave me was just an estimate. If the rate turned out to be higher, I would have had to pay that extra money, no matter how much higher, within 15 days after completion of the move.

The moving company will give you only a limited time (in my case they allowed only 7 days) before they will start adding extra storage and handling charges. Since I had no idea where I would be living when I arrived in Norman, Oklahoma, my bill could well have mounted up to $3,000 if it took me too long to find a place to live.

There are some special and unusual items to keep in mind if you hire a mover. I was shocked to find out that the mover would charge 19.6 cents a pound to move my things. Books can be sent, fourth class, for 66¢ for the first two pounds and 11 cents for each additional pound. So, you can mail a box of books of the maximum amount permitted (70 pounds) for $8.45. The moving company will charge you almost double that, or $13.34

Another problem with using moving companies is that they are not always able to guarantee a pickup and delivery on a specific day since they often carry up to about 6 households of furniture on one truck. You may have to wait to have your furniture picked up and to have your furniture delivered at your destination for a few days.

IF YOU MOVE YOURSELF

First of all check with 2 or 3 do–it–yourself moving companies and get all their booklets and rates so you can make an intelligent comparison. They'll also give you check lists so you can go through your house and check the cubic footage of what you have to move so you can select the right sized truck. You'll also have the estimates from the moving companies to double check what size truck you'll need. If in doubt, rent the next size larger, the difference in cost isn't much.

Figure 10-1 is the basic comparison chart I made before I rented a truck for my move.

DO-IT-YOURSELF COMPARISON CHART

		Company A	Company B	Company C
1.	Length	24 feet	24 feet	22 feet
2.	Capacity in cubic feet	1,150	1,100	1,200
3.	Base rate	$550	$626	$763
4.	Mileage	1,475	1,499	1,465
5.	Days	7	6	6
6.	Rate per extra mile	$.25	$.25	$.25
7.	Rate per extra day	$25	$25	$25
8.	Insurance	$20	$35	$20
9.	Hand truck or dolly	$5	None	$7
10.	Foam pads for furniture, cost per dozen	$5	None	$7
11.	Tow bar	$39	None	$40
12.	Redistribution Charge	$325	None	None

Figure 10-1

Lines 1 and 2 give the length and capacity of the rental truck. A 24 foot van truck is the largest normally available, but you can add a trailer to this truck and end up with about 1600 cubic feet of carrying capacity. Smaller trucks, down to 12 feet, with about 550 cubic feet, are available as are a wide variety of trailers from about 100 to 500 cubic feet.

The base rate reflected in lines 4, 5, and 6 is determined from the renter's mileage charts. In this case I was allowed to travel 1475 miles and to keep the truck for a total of 7 days without incurring additional charges. I selected Company A because of their lower cost and because of their nationally known reputation. For extra mileage (above 1475 miles) and for extra days (over 7 days) the charges are as indicated on lines 6 and 7. The insurance covers your household goods and certain accident and medical benefits for you. I consider it a necessity.

You'll need a handtruck to move your refrigerator, your washer and dryer and whatever else is too heavy to carry directly. A dolly is a necessity in a move.

I rented 4 dozen foam pads. Next time I'll rent 8 dozen. They're inexpensive and very useful.

With a tow bar you can pull your car behind the truck and save the gas required to power 2 vehicles separately. Also you'll eliminate the possibility of 2 drivers getting lost or separated in the middle of nowhere.

Incidentally, I found out I could purchase a tow bar for $30, $9 less than I could rent one for. So I bought a tow bar for pulling my VW.

To rent a truck, you'll have to make about a $50 deposit a few days ahead of time. Then you'll have to pay in cash or certified check the estimated cost of the move, before you get the truck.

You pay for all the gas, the rental company pays for the oil and any needed repairs on the trip. Some states require trip permits, some have tolls. You pay for these also.

The maximum speed on the rental truck is usually 50 miles per hour, set by a governor on the truck. And you'll be driving a lot slower up hills than with a regular car. Don't drive at night. It's 4 times as dangerous as daytime driving and not worth the time you think you'll save.

Another item to watch out for is called a *redistribution charge.* It so happens that more people are moving into a certain area than leave. So that area ends up with a surplus of one–way, do–it–yourself moving trucks. The company has to hire people to drive these trucks to other areas, so they may sock you with a redistribution charge.

On my move from California to Oklahoma, I was supposed to be assessed a $325 redistribution charge. But I found out that no redistribution charge was assessed if I delivered the truck to eastern Kansas. After I unloaded my goods in Norman, Oklahoma I drove the truck and left it in eastern Kansas just over the border and saved the $325.

Check with your renter to see if they have such a charge. You may be able to avoid it by doing what I did.

Using Figure 10-2, figure out what your do–it–yourself move will cost. Compare it with what your moving company estimated. Then you can make an intelligent decision on how to move.

MOVING COST ESTIMATE

	Cost
Basic rate _____ Miles	_____
Gasoline _____ Miles _____ ¢ per mile	_____
Insurance	_____
Hand Truck	_____
Foam pads $ _____ per dozen ____ dozen	_____
Tow bar, if needed	_____
Packing crates	_____
Miscellaneous: tapes, ropes, etc. (allow at least $10)	_____
TOTAL	==========

Figure 10-2

HOW TO PACK YOURSELF

If you're moving yourself or if you're having your things moved and are doing the packing to save some money, most of the following information will be of benefit to you. Even if you're moving only a short distance a great deal will apply, although you won't have to take such elaborate precautions.

One fundamental rule of packing is to try to keep each and every box under 50 pounds in weight. You don't want to hurt yourself toting heavier boxes.

Where do you get boxes? You can buy them from the moving companies, from companies which specialize in selling boxes or from the do–it–yourself moving van company. This is an expensive route to take.

There are many places you can get free boxes. It's going to take a lot of boxes so start collecting them early. I found out that certain grocery stores were very helpful in supplying most of my moving cartons. We found that the most useful boxes were the heavy, corrugated boxes grocery stores receive and store their fruit in. These are 2 piece boxes with a full height and overlapping cover which gives you a lot of protection for the contents.

Another excellent source is the local liquor store. They receive their bottles of liquor in boxes with cardboard dividers inside. These corrugated boxes with the cushioned dividers are excellent for packing glasses, bottles, vases and dozens of other items after you have first wrapped them with tissue or newspaper. You can also get these partitioned boxes from grocery stores where they receive glass container items. Call the local grocery stores and some liquor stores and ask them on which days they have the most boxes, when they restore their inventory, restock their shelves. Ask them to save them for you. They'll usually accomodate you and you can get most of your needed boxes this way.

Wardrobe boxes are necessary. You'll probably have to buy a couple for your clothes. And you might consider buying a fiber barrel or 2 for packing larger itmes.

When you must pack heavy boxes, each person should carry no more than 75 pounds. So keep this in mind if you try to lift a 150 pound box by yourself. You may not be able to straighten up again.

As far as the time required to pack, you should allow as long as possible. A month of spare time if you have it. If you're in a hurry, you should be able to do it in a week.

Another fundamental rule of packing is to put the heavier things on the bottom of the box and load them on the bottom of the truck, also. Wrap all items individually. Even non–breakables can rub against each other on a 1000 mile trip and damage each other. Provide plenty of cushioning. Make sure things are packed firmly together by stuffing in newspapers, old clothes, etc. On a long trip the body of a moving truck can move about a lot and things can get bounced around.

Label all boxes both on the top and the sides so that, once they're stacked on the truck, you can read the labels. Label them with notes such as *kitchen utensils*, *Sandy's dolls*, *spices*, etc. so you'll know exactly where they'll go when you unload, and how to load them on the truck. Put the clothes you normally hang in your closet in wardrobes using hangers. For clothes you normally keep in your bureau drawers, leave them there. Bureau drawers are also good places for packing certain other breakable items, such as small mirrors, pictures, etc. Cushion these breakables between clothing.

Old newspapers, towels, blankets make good cushions. Keep these handy to wedge into spaces you need to fill in to make a good, firm pack in each box.

DISHES

Here's your trickiest item. Glasses and dishes should be wrapped in 3 layers of paper. However, if they're good quality, wrap them in one layer of tissue paper first, then 2 layers of newspaper because the newsprint can come off and imprint your good china. Glasses pack well in the liquor cartons, between the dividers.

Pack dishes up on end, padding underneath them and on their sides. Stuff newspapers and dishtowels to make a firm pack. Bowls and such can be stacked as long as they're cushioned with newspaper or tissue paper.

If you are especially nervous and concerned about your good dishes and glassware, you could hire a professional packer. A professional will use special boxes and pack them carefully so there's little possibility of damage. The charge for a typical kitchen, for good dishes, would be about $40.

For kitchen utensils again pack the heavy items on the bottom, the lighter on top. Wrap them individually, interweave layers and adjacent items with paper also.

Get rid of all perishable foods, tape closed any open food packages or cartons. Cover heads of shakers with tape.

BOOKS

Pack books in small, rectangular cartons. Books weigh an average of 1 pound so don't count on packing more than about 40 to 50 books in one carton. Pack them lying on their covers. If they're valuable books, wrap them up in tissue paper individually. I found the apple boxes excellent for books.

TABLES AND APPLIANCES

If possible take the legs off the tables and wrap everything in foam pads. They'll take up much less space and will less likely be damaged.

Clean out your refrigerator 1 or 2 days before you move. Defrost it, wash it and let it dry out with the door open. The tub in your washer should be braced so it doesn't shift around and bang against the insides. Slip some heavy pieces of cardboard or some heavy fabric (e.g. towels, throw rugs, etc.) around the edges of the tub to anchor it into place. And you can put some light-weight soft things, such as pillows, stuffed animals, etc. to load up the inside of the washer tub and your dryer drum. Use all of the space you have as efficiently as possible.

Cover your TV set completely and liberally with foam pads, especially the picture tube at the front. The turntable and the playing arm of your stereo or record player should be taped in place so it can't move. Store records in their jackets up on end in relatively small boxes and mark them fragile. Records are very heavy if you try to crowd too many into a large box.

SPECIAL ITEMS

If you have an old piano give serious thought before moving it. A piano weighs a few hundred pounds and takes quite a few pairs of muscles to handle it. If you're going to carry it up to a second floor apartment at your destination, well, good luck. Maybe you should sell it or donate it to charity and buy another used one at your new destination.

Drapes can be folded and will fit at the bottoms of the wardrobe containers. Shoes can also be put at the bottoms of the wardrobes. A large lamp shade can be placed alone at the bottom of a filled clothing wardrobe, or they should be placed in cartons by themselves and marked fragile.

Lamp bases, if large, should be wrapped in foam pads. Mirrors, pictures, etc.: you can pack the smaller ones firmly between the layers of clothing in your dressers. Larger ones should be sandwiched between layers of good, heavy, corrugated cardboard and taped together, labeled as glass and loaded in a specially cushioned place in the van, possibly between a pair of mattresses.

You can buy mattress boxes or cover them with foam pads. They also make excellent cushions to put between such items as a couple of dressers you don't want to rub against each other.

Bundle your garden tools together. We found an old 50 gallon fiber barrel which handled our garden tools, hoses, etc. very nicely.

HOW TO LOAD THE VAN

We rented the cab–over–van and found the space over the cab an ideal place to load our mattresses.

In general, for loading, put the heavier items on the bottom, the lighter and fragile items on the top. The floor of your van will be loaded with such heavies as your washer, dressers, etc. After covering these items with pads, put your lighter boxes on top of them. Keep piling lighter and lighter boxes on top until you reach the ceiling of the van.

It's best to alternate your loading so that, for example, you put your refrigerator and washer in one row, stick pads all around them. Then fill up the next vertical row with boxes of books. Also, once the heavy items, such as the washer, are loaded they should be anchored down with ropes running back and forth between the tie rings provided inside the van. This will keep them from moving or shifting during transit.

As you load you'll find empty spaces under tables, between major items, etc. Stuff your heavier boxes in those spaces, not only to conserve space, but also to prevent movement of your heavier items. Wedge pillows, foam pads, etc. in all holes to make a firm pack.

When you load dressers take all of the drawers out. Carry the empty dresser on to the truck, put it in place and then replace the full drawers in the dresser.

Every few feet of length, run anchor ropes back and forth through the rings provided. Rope is a cheap and worthwhile investment to insure a damage–free shipment.

Pack any items you figure you'll need first when you get to your new location near the back of the truck for easy access. For example, you may want to pack a few cans of soup, some crackers, and a couple of pots and pans and dishes which you can get to when you get hungry and haven't got time to unpack the entire truck.

Keep a record of all your expenses. Under certain conditions, these expenses are deductible from your income tax.

IF YOU HIRE A MOVER

You have to give a mover about 2 weeks notice or they won't be able to give you an exact delivery date for your items at the other end. Even so they may miss it by a day or 2, or perhaps longer.

If the mover packs your things, they may come in 1 or 2 days ahead of the estimate. Packing costs are typically $6 per 100 pounds. If you intend to use a mover but do your own packing be sure you do a good job. If the mover doesn't think you've packed properly he can reject what he considers an improperly packed shipment and repack it, at your expense.

One rule of thumb for movers is that for 6 rooms or less, assume 1200 pounds are to be moved per room. For over 6 rooms, an estimate used is 1500 pounds per room.

There are some things a mover won't transport. Among them are plants, pets, valuables, important papers, flammables, pressurized cans, ammunition, paint, fuel oil, and many other similar items.

ARE MOVING EXPENSES TAX DEDUCTIBLE?

For moving expenses to be tax deductible, certain criteria must be met. If your move is caused by a change in the location of your employment, either as a transfer by your present employer, or your acceptance of a new job, you can deduct reasonable expenses if:

1. Your new job location makes you commute 50 miles farther to work.
2. You move within 1 year of the time you start work at the new location.
3. You work full–time (39 weeks during the next 12 month period) at the new location. If you're self–employed, you must work 78 weeks, of which 39 must be in the first 12 months after moving.

For more information on this subject, request a free copy of the Internal Revenue Service Publication 512 entitled *Tax Information and Moving Expenses.* Or you can pick up a copy at the local post office. See your income tax accountant for further details concerning these deductions.

TAX CONSIDERATIONS

Hopefully you've sold your house for more than you paid for it. This profit is called *Capital Gains* if you've held this property for longer than 12 months. One half of this profit must be added to your income for the current year and declared as income. Or, if you purchase another house for the same or higher price, you can postpone payment of this capital gains tax.

I can sketch only briefly the basic considerations on this law. For a complete discussion request the booklet *Tax Information on Selling Your Home* publication 523 from the local Internal Revenue Service.

Some of the work you've done while living in the house are capital improvements and may be deducted from this capital gains profit. Also, some of the selling costs can be deducted. In general, consider the following:

1. Legal fees in selling your house are deductible.
2. Any capital improvements, such as a swimming pool, additional room, etc. are deductible from this profit.
3. Normal maintenance costs are not deductible.
4. Advertising costs incurred in selling your own home are deductible.
5. In general most closing costs, both when you originally bought the house and when you sold the house, are deductible from your profits.

Keep receipts of all the work you've done and all of the capital improvements you've made. See your income tax adviser for further help in this complex matter. It's worth the investment. Unfortunately, if you suffer a loss in the sale of a house, you can't deduct this loss from your income.

POSTPONING THE TAX

There are ways, however, for postponing the payment of this capital gains tax.

If you purchase a house which costs more than the one you sold within 18 months, you can postpone paying this capital gains tax. In addition to the deductible expenses mentioned under the preceding paragraphs, any work you have done on your old residence to assist its sale (e.g. fixing up expenses, such as painting your house, installing a new water heater, etc.), if performed within 90 days of the sale and paid for within 30 days of the sale, can be used to figure out your adjusted sales price. The adjusted sales price is effectively the price the government calculated that you netted on the sale of your house. So, if you buy a house which costs more than this adjusted sales price, you will be postponing paying this tax. The formula and further details of this situation are amply covered in the Infernal Revenue Service pamphlet 523 mentioned earlier.

$100,000 Once-In-A-Lifetime Exclusion

If you're over 55 and are selling your house, you can exclude up to $100,000 of the profit you make on the sale. To qualify, you must have owned and used the house as your principal residence for a total of at least three years prior to the sale. (This also applies to a condominium or stock of a shareholder-tenant of a cooperative housing corporation). You can use this exemption only once-in-a-lifetime.

As an example, suppose you are 58 years old and want to sell your house. You paid $25,000 for it ten years ago and now you sell it for $125,000. You will pay capital gains tax on:

Sale cost of house	$125,000
Minus initial cost of house	$25,000
Minus once-in-a-lifetime exclusion	$100,000
	-0-

You need pay *no* capital gains tax if your profit is $100,000 or less.

The example I've given is a simple one. On an investment of this magnitude, by all means contact a competent tax attorney or an accountant for help in figuring out your specific situation.

GOOD LUCK AND DON'T FORGET TO WRITE

I sincerely hope this book has been a big help to you in selling your own home and pocketing the profits. You'll find it a rewarding experience, frustrating at times, but overall you'll look back on it fondly and with a great deal of justifiable pride.

You've sold your house, all by yourself. That's much more than many people accomplish in an entire lifetime.

Good luck, and don't forget to write me, in care of my publisher, to tell me how this book helped you and how later editions of it can be improved.

GLOSSARY OF REAL ESTATE TERMS

ABSTRACT OF TITLE A brief history of the previous ownership of property, including all liens or encumbrances and any claims against the property. This does not give title to a property.

ACRE A measure of land area which equals 43,560 square feet. A square acre lot would measure about 210 by 210 feet.

AD VALOREM In Latin—*According to value.* Your property is taxed according to value. The more your real estate is worth, the higher your taxes.

AGREEMENT OF SALE or PURCHASE AND SALE AGREEMENT Agreement means the same as Contract. *See* CONTRACT OF SALE.

AMENITIES Natural or man–made attractions which increase the value of property such as trees, nearby parks, a beautiful view, etc.

AMORTIZATION Paying off a loan, in installments (usually equal monthly payments). The payments are made large enough to pay both interest and part of the principal, so the debt is gradually reduced and completely paid off at the end of the loan period.

APPRAISAL An estimate of the value of a property on a certain date.

APPRAISER An expert who, for a fee, estimates the value of property.

APPRECIATION An increase in the value of property caused by changes in economic conditions, improvements in the neighborhood, etc. The opposite of depreciation.

APPURTENANCES Property rights, privileges or improvements. Although they are not strictly a part of the land, they go with the title to the new owner, such as easements, right of way, orchards, etc.

ASSESSED VALUE The value placed on real estate by the tax assessor to determine the amount of taxes on the property. Assessed value is often some fraction (as low as 1/4 to 1/5) of the market value of the property.

ASSESSMENT A government imposed tax for a specific purpose such as a street improvement, a sewer, etc. The assessment is levied against those who benefit mostly from the improvement.

BENCH MARK A permanently fixed marker in the ground, such as a metal marker, which surveyors use to establish property lines and elevation. Also called a monument.

BINDER A short term agreement by which the buyer and seller tentatively agree on the terms of a contract.

BROKER A person licensed by the state who sells real estate for a commission. A broker is usually hired by a seller.

BUILDING CODES Local rules which regulate the construction of buildings, such as size, location and uses of buildings.

CARRYING CHARGES The money it costs to own property including mortgage payments, insurance, taxes and maintenance. This is equivalent of rent one would pay for an apartment or house.

CAVEAT EMPTOR *Let the Buyer Beware.* The buyer purchases real estate in an *as is* condition and must investigate and take the risks which go with any purchase. The seller cannot be held responsible for the quality of the property unless guaranteed in a warranty.

CHATTEL MORTGAGE A mortgage on personal property.

CHATTELS *See personal property.*

CLOSING COSTS The miscellaneous charges, over and above the cost of the house, paid by the buyer and the seller at escrow closing, when the deed to the property is transferred from the seller to the buyer.

COLLATERAL   Security (e.g. bonds, jewelry, or other marketable items) pledged for payment of a loan.

COMMITMENT   A promise made by a lender to make a specific loan to a specific person.

COMMUNITY PROPERTY   Property acquired by a husband, a wife, or by both together which is considered to be jointly owned and equally shared. Community property laws are valid in only a few states.

CONTRACT OF SALE   A legally enforceable, written agreement where the buyer agrees to purchase and the seller agrees to sell certain real estate in accordance with the conditions written into the agreement. Both parties to the agreement must be competent (this excludes minors and people of unsound mind).

CONVENTIONAL LOAN   A mortgage which is not insured by the FHA nor guaranteed by the VA. The loan rates and conditions are set by the lender (subject to limited controls by the government). The real property is used as security for the loan.

CONVEYANCE   The transfer of ownership of real estate by deed from one party to another.

COVENANT   A promise or agreement between two parties usually applied to specific promises in a deed. A *contract* can be thought of as an exchange of *covenants*.

CUBIC FEET   A measure of volume of an object, a room, container, etc. it is obtained by multiplying the length, height and width (all in feet). This measure is used as the capacity of a moving van, of a box or of any container.

DEED   A document which describes property and is used to transfer ownership of that property.

DEED OF TRUST   Used in some states in place of a

mortgage. The buyer deeds the property to a third party (usually a title or escrow company) who holds the deed in trust to guarantee that the buyer will repay the loan to the lender.

DEFAULT   The failure to meet a promise on a contract, including not paying money when due, or not complying with ohter provisions of the contract.

DEPOSIT   A small downpayment given by the buyer when the buyer makes an offer to purchase. The deposit may become the *earnest money* when the contract is signed, or the buyer may have to add money to the deposit to constitute the *earnest money.*

DEPRECIATION   The decrease in value of property caused by age, wear and tear, and changing neighborhood conditions, etc. Opposite of appreciation.

DOCUMENTARY STAMPS   State tax stamps charged and affixed to a mortgage note and deed.

DOWN PAYMENT   The money a buyer must pay in cash on a house before being granted a loan.

EARNEST MONEY   A payment made as evidence of a serious buyer's intent to go through with the purchase of real estate, often 10 percent of the purchase price. It is given by the buyer on the signing of a contract for the sale of real estate. If the buyer defaults in carrying out the contract, the money may be forfeited to the seller.

EASEMENT   The right of a person to use someone else's land for a particular purpose. For example, a utility company may have the right to enter, install and service utility lines on the property. These easements become a part of the deed and are transferred to the new owner each time the land is sold.

EMINENT DOMAIN   The right of the government to take over part or all of a person's property for public use. This may be done with or without the owner's consent. The government must pay the owner the fair price for this property.

ENCROACHMENT   A trespass or invasion over the property line of another person, such as a fence, a building overhang, etc.

ENCUMBRANCE   Any claim or lien on real estate, such as a mortgage, court judgment, unpaid taxes, etc. These show up during the *title search*. Unpaid taxes and judgments must be paid before transferring title.

EQUITY   The interest or value an owner has in real estate over and above the remaining mortgage. The equity is the difference between the selling price of the house and the unpaid mortgage.

ESCALATION CLAUSE   A clause written into some loan agreements which permits the lender to raise or lower the interest rate, without the borrower's consent, as business conditions change.

ESCROW   A third, neutral party which holds and processes documents, initiates necessary paperwork, collects money due, pays out money due, etc. Escrow insures that both parties meet all aspects of the agreement before permitting title to pass from seller to buyer.

ET AL   Legal doubletalk for *and others*.

FEE SIMPLE   Ownership of real estate, free from all conditions and limitations. Complete ownership of land.

FIRST MORTGAGE   The principal mortgage that is the first lien on the property. This has first claim (after delinquent taxes, if any) on the money realized in a foreclosure.

FHA MORTGAGE   A mortgage, given by a commercial lender, which is insured by the Federal Housing Administration. The FHA sets the interest rates and downpayments and assesses an insurance fee from the buyer (1/2 percent) to insure repayment of the

loan in case of default. The FHA makes low downpayment loans available to lower income, qualified
buyers.

FIXTURE   Personal property which has become real
property because it's attached to the real property, or
agreed by both parties to pass with the property, or
because of local custom.

FORECLOSURE   When a lender, by legal proceedings,
forces the sale of a mortgaged property to recover the
loan money remaining when a borrower defaults on a
loan.

GI MORTGAGE   *See* VA mortgage.

GRANTEE   The buyer of real estate. The term often
used in a deed.

GRANTOR   The seller of real estate. The term often used
in a deed.

GUARANTY   A promise to answer for performance of an
obligation.

HOMESTEAD   Real Estate occupied by the owner as a
home has *homestead rights*, special privileges such as
homestead tax exemptions, an exemption from certain
claims of creditors, etc.

INTEREST   Money paid for borrowing money, usually
expressed in percent. It may cost, for example, $10 to
borrow $100 at a 10 percent interest rate for 1 year.

JOINT TENANCY   Property jointly owned by 2 or more
persons. Each can assume full title to the property if
the other dies. It avoids probate.

LIEN   A hold or legal claim a person has on the property
of another as security for a debt (such as a mortgage,
mechanics lien, unpaid taxes, etc.) and for which the
property can be sold to settle that debt.

MARKET VALUE The amount buyers will pay for a given property at a given time. The value of property on an open market.

MARKETABLE TITLE A title to a property, not completely clear, but with only minor objections which a court would require a buyer to accept.

MECHANIC'S LIEN A hold or claim on the property of another as security for an unpaid bill of a building contractor, material supplier, or workman.

MORTGAGE A loan in which buyer pledges the real estate as security of repayment. This lien on the property continues until the loan has been paid off.

MORTGAGE The institution which lends the money.

MORTGAGOR The person who borrows the money, using property as security.

NOTE A written agreement sometimes secured by a mortgage by which the borrower acknowledges the debt and promises to pay it in a specified time. A home buyer usually signs a note as well as a mortgage at closing. Also called a promissory note.

OFFER A dcoument signed by the buyer offering to buy certain real estate at a specific price. The signed acceptance of the seller makes it a contract if all the essential items are covered. It lists the price and conditions under which the buyer agrees to purchase the property.

OPEN END MORTGAGE A mortgage having a clause which permits the home owner to refinance the mortgage in the future to raise funds without having to rewrite the mortgage and pay closing costs again.

OPTION The right to buy property at a specified price within a stated time. If the owner receives consideration (e.g. money) the owner is bound to honor the option.

ORIGINATION AND PROCESSING FEES Fees lenders

charge for granting a mortgage and processing a loan. May include points if money is tight.

PERSONAL PROPERTY All types of moveable, tangible items which people can own.

PLAT A map showing the planned use of land.

POINTS A one-time special charge a lender makes for giving a loan, over and above the interest rate. 1 point is 1 percent of the mortgage value, i.e. $10 for each $1000 borrowed.

PREPAYMENT PENALTY Some lenders charge a penalty if a borrower pays off a long term loan ahead of time.

PRINCIPAL The amount of the mortgage remaining to be paid at any particular time. The principal continually decreases as loan payments are made, reaching zero when the loan is paid off.

PROMISSORY NOTE *see* note

QUIT CLAIM DEED It transfers title of property without warranties. It conveys whatever interest the owner has in the property. The buyer is responsible for any claims brought against the property.

REAL PROPERTY or REAL ESTATE The land and everything built or growing on it, or attached to it.

REALTOR A person licensed by the state to sell real estate and who is also a member of the National Association of Realtors and lives up to a strict code of ethics which protect both the buyer and the seller.

RECORDING Placing a transaction into the public records at the county courthouse.

RESTRICTIVE COVENANT An agreement limiting the use of property. It is usually undertaken by neighborhood property owners to preserve open space or to prevent undesirable businesses or non-residential activities.

SECOND MORTGAGE A mortgage given in addition to

the first mortgage. The holder of the second mortgage has second priority on the funds realized in case of a foreclosure and sale of the property.

SETBACK   The distance (specified by a zoning ordinance or restriction) that must be left between a building and the boundaries of the lot. Also the distance from any building to the curb.

SQUARE FOOTAGE   A measure of area. Mulitply the length times the width (both in feet) to obtain the square footage, or living space of a room or house.

SURVEY   The process of determining the precise location and boundaries of a piece of land.

TENDER   An offer of money.

TITLE   Proof of ownership of real estate.

TITLE INSURANCE   A policy written by a title company which guarantees the title to property. If the title becomes clouded because of a claim of prior ownership by someone else the title company must make good any losses arising from these defects.

TITLE SEARCH   An examination of public records to find out the history of ownership of property. It determines legal status of property.

TRANSFER   A change of ownership of property.

TRUST DEED   See deed of trust.

USURY   Interest rates charged in excess of that permitted by law.

VA MORTGAGE   A mortgage made by a commercial lender, but under rules and regulations established by the Veterans' Administration. Available to veterans, the interest rate is regulated by the government and payment is guaranteed by the government up to a certain amount in case of default. Characterized by no down payment or low-downpayment loans.

VALUATION   An estimate of a property's worth.

VENDEE   The buyer of real estate.
VENDOR   The seller of real estate

WAIVER   Voluntarily giving up a claim, right or privilege.
WARRANTY   A guarantee by the seller that the title is conveyed as stated in the deed.

ZONING   Municipal laws which regulate the uses to which land can be put.

INDEX

House

8.6
12
2
___
14
9
___

24
30'

30'
22"2
GARAGE

32 HOUSE
48